THE
COUNTRY
HOUSE
AT WAR

THE
COUNTRY
HOUSE
AT WAR

John Martin Robinson

THE BODLEY HEAD
LONDON

ACKNOWLEDGEMENTS

The passages quoted from *Brideshead Revisited, Put out More Flags* and *Men at Arms* are reprinted by permission of the Peters Fraser & Dunlop Group Ltd. The quotations from Evelyn Waugh's diaries are from *The Diaries of Evelyn Waugh* edited by Michael Davie and published by Weidenfeld & Nicolson (1976).

Thanks to the following copyright holders for the use of illustrative material: Trustees of the Chatsworth Settlement 1, 3; Courtauld Institute of Art and the Trustees of the Chatsworth Settlement 2; Yorkshire Post 4; Malvern College 5, 6; National Monuments Record 7, 8, 13, 36, 37, 38, 39, 40, 41, 42; The Marquess of Salisbury 9, 10; The Duke of Norfolk 11; National Portrait Gallery 12; National Gallery 14; Imperial War Museum 15, 16, 17, 19, 20, 21, 22, 23, 24, 25, 26, 27, 28, 29, 30, 31, 32; Derby Museum 34. Cartoons on pages 3, 19, 71, 83, 105, 129 and 155 reproduced by permission of *Punch*.

A CIP catalogue record for this book is
available from the British Library

ISBN 0–370–31306–2

© John Martin Robinson 1989

Printed and bound in
Great Britain for
The Bodley Head Ltd
31 Bedford Square
London WC1B 3SG
by Mackays of Chatham PLC
set in Bembo
by Falcon Graphic Art Ltd
Wallington, Surrey

First published 1989

Contents

Author's Note		vi
Prologue		vii
Introduction		1
Chapter I	The Grand Plan	3
Chapter II	Evacuees	19
Chapter III	Schools	39
Chapter IV	Hospitals	71
Chapter V	Museums	83
Chapter VI	Intelligence	105
Chapter VII	The Armed Forces	129
Chapter VIII	Damage and Destruction	155
Appendix	*Compensation Defence Act, 1939*	
	2 & 3 Geo.6 c.43	174
Index		179

Author's Note

I am grateful to the following people and institutions who have given me their time and access to their records in order to provide so much of the material of this book:

Steven M. Atkin; Peter Avery; Mrs U.A. Aylmer; Commander and Mrs Andrew Baird; R.E. Bishop; Christopher Brown; The Trustees of the Chatsworth Settlement; David Clegg; Courtauld Institute; Maxwell Craven; Peter Day; Duchess of Devonshire; Marie Draper; The Commander, HMS *Dryad*; Brian Fothergill; Christopher Gattiss; Robin Harcourt-Williams; Eeyan Hartley; Dr W.O. Hassall; Richard Hewlings; Mrs J. Hext; Imperial War Museum; A.R. Kibblewhite; David Laws; James Lees-Milne; Jonathon Miles; Philip Miles; James Money; Hugh Montgomery-Massingberd; National Monuments Record; National Portrait Gallery (with reservations); Duke of Norfolk; Mrs J.F. Parsons; Miss Rachel Pool; Public Records Office; Peter Reid; Lt Commander Ian Rodger; The Marquess of Salisbury; Ian Scott; Mr and Mrs Y.C. Sell; Gavin Stamp; David Twiston-Davies; David Watkin; Mrs Gilbert Woods.

JMR
London 1989

Prologue

I asked the second-in-command, 'What's this place called?'

He told me and, on the instant, it was as though someone had switched off the wireless, and a voice that had been bawling in my ears, incessantly, fatuously, for days beyond number, had been suddenly cut short; an immense silence followed, empty at first, but gradually, as my outraged sense regained authority, full of a multitude of sweet and natural and long forgotten sounds: for he had spoken a name that was so familiar to me, a conjuror's name of such ancient power, that, at its mere sound, the phantoms of those haunted late years began to take flight.

Outside the hut I stood bemused. The rain had ceased but the clouds hung low and heavy overhead. It was a still morning and the smoke from the cookhouse rose straight to the leaden sky. A cart-track, once metalled, then overgrown, now rutted and churned to mud, followed the contour of the hillside and dipped out of sight below a knoll, and on either side of it lay the haphazard litter of corrugated iron, from which rose the rattle and chatter and whistling and catcalls, all the zoo-noises of the battalion beginning a new day. Beyond and about us, more familiar still, lay an exquisite manmade landscape. It was a sequestered place, enclosed and embraced in a single, winding valley. Our camp lay along one gentle slope; opposite us the ground led, still unravished, to the neighbourly horizon, and between us flowed a stream — it was named the Bride and rose not two miles away at a farm called Bridesprings, where we used sometimes to walk to tea; it became a considerable river lower down before it joined the Avon — which had been dammed here to form three lakes, one no more than a wet slate among the reeds, but the others more spacious, reflecting the clouds and the mighty beeches at their margin. The woods were all of oak and beech, the oak grey and bare, the beech faintly dusted with green by the breaking buds; they made a simple, carefully designed pattern with the green glades and the wide green spaces – Did the fallow deer graze here still? – and, lest the eye wander aimlessly, a Doric temple stood by the water's edge, and an ivy-grown arch spanned the lowest of the connecting weirs. All this had been planned and planted a century and a half ago so that, at about this date, it might be seen in its maturity. From where I stood the house was hidden by a green spur, but I knew well how and where it lay, couched among the lime trees like a hind in the bracken.

Hooper came sidling up and greeted me with his much imitated but inimitable salute. His face was grey from his night's vigil and he had not yet shaved.

' "B" Company relieved us. I've sent the chaps off to get cleaned up.'

'Good.'

'The house is up there, round the corner.'

'Yes,' I said.

'Brigade Headquarters are coming there next week. Great barrack of a place. I've just had a snoop round. Very ornate, I'd call it. And a queer thing, there's a sort of R.C. Church attached. I looked in and there was a kind of service going on – just a padre and one old man. I felt very awkward. More in your line than mine.' Perhaps I seemed not to hear; in a final effort to excite my interest he said: 'There's a frightful great fountain, too, in front of the steps, all rocks and sort of carved animals. You never saw such a thing.'

'Yes, Hooper, I did. I've been here before.'

Evelyn Waugh, Brideshead Revisited

Introduction

One of the most interesting and dramatic episodes in the history of the English country house is its role during the Second World War, when the majority of houses of large size in Britain were requisitioned by the government, or donated by their owners, for use as schools, barracks, hostels for evacuees, hospitals, convalescent homes, intelligence, strategic and military headquarters, billets and training premises for the armed forces, and even as prisoner-of-war camps. Several great houses had been part-occupied as convalescent homes or military hospitals during the First World War, including Blenheim, Hatfield, Woburn and Longleat, but such a use had been more the result of the spontaneous generosity and patriotism of their owners, than of any government decree. During the Second World War, though some houses were made immediately available by leading members of the peerage for a specific purpose, the majority were compulsorily requisitioned by the government and put to a multitude of uses. The houses so occupied were of immense value on the home front and formed a characteristic aspect of the total mobilisation of the nation, both state and private resources, in the British war effort.

In purely organisational terms, it represented a remarkable achievement. Indeed, several houses played a special role in the history of the Second

World War. Southwick Park in Hampshire, for instance, served as the Headquarters for Supreme Allied Command prior to D-Day. Wilton House, near Salisbury, was the Headquarters of Southern Command throughout the war. Merton Hall, and its estate, in Norfolk was used for the training of Montgomery's forces for the Normandy landings, and Woburn Abbey was the country Headquarters of the Foreign Office Intelligence Unit.

The wartime occupation of country houses was not, however, without sacrifice. Though comparatively few English country houses were destroyed as a direct result of enemy action, a very considerable number were irreparably damaged by their new tenants; several being burnt to the ground. Many more were left in such poor condition in 1945 that they proved incapable of restoration. The thousand or so country houses demolished in the decade after the end of the Second World War were nearly all delayed war losses. The destruction of the country house brought about by its occupation and hard usage during the Second World War, while not as thoroughgoing as the dissolution of the monasteries in the sixteenth century, can only be paralleled in English cultural history by the architectural losses of the Reformation. Despite that, there is a resourcefulness, an exhilaration, a sense of achievement in this unique contribution to the war effort that, to coin a phrase, marks the five years between 1939 and 1945 as the country house's 'finest hour'.

Chapter I
The Grand Plan

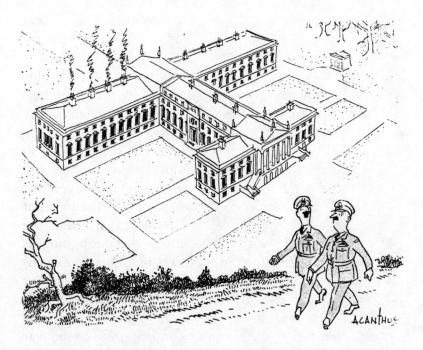

"Once they occupied the fuselage, but of course now they can only afford one wing."

It became increasingly clear from the mid-1930s onwards that armed conflict with Hitler's Germany was inevitable. The British government, belatedly, began to plan for the mobilisation of the nation when war broke out. This involved, as well as building up the armed forces, far-reaching plans for the 'home front'. At a meeting of the Committee of Imperial Defence on 15 April 1937, it was decided that surveys should be undertaken in all parts of the country of buildings which could be utilised in the war effort. Overall control of this survey and responsibility for the central register was entrusted to the Office of Works, under the direction of E.N. de Normann. He headed the Directorate of Lands and Accommodation, based in London but in control of a local network of Office of Works representatives to whom was delegated much of the survey work. The register itself was begun in May 1938. It was divided initially into four categories: London Postal Areas; English Counties (including Northern Ireland and the Channel Islands); Welsh Counties; and Scottish Counties. However, once under way a more specific regional breakdown was adopted instead.

The register was intended to ensure that the buildings needed for war purposes would be available for occupation when required, and also to prevent the overlapping of demands and conflicts between different government departments and, to a lesser degree, local authorities, which it was envisaged would have requisitioning powers for civil defence purposes under the Air Raid Precautions (ARP) act. On 22 March 1938, the Treasury sent out a circular letter to all government departments informing them that an earmarking procedure was to be adopted, and explaining that premises could not be requisitioned for war purposes unless they had been reserved previously by the department concerned. Though slow at first, there was a positive response, with a flood of earmarkings pouring in during the months immediately before and after the outbreak of war.

The government departments invited to contribute to the register were the War Office, the Admiralty, the Air Ministry, the Ministry of Transport, the Board of Trade, the Food (Defence Plans) Department, the Office of Works, the Ministry of Health, the Board of Customs and Excise, the Home Office, the Air Raid Precautions Department, the Board of Education and the Scottish Office. The Board of Education in its initial submission to E.N. de Normann on 15 September 1938 had stated that 'We shall not be requisitioning any premises in the event of war', though later it did compile a list of earmarked properties.

The plans for requisitioning, hitherto rather sketchy and unreal, suddenly found themselves in earnest during the Munich crisis in September 1938 when it seemed that war might break out immediately. A conference of the heads of divisions in the civil service formally agreed to a series of measures to be adopted in the case of an 'emergency'. First, the requisitioning of accommodation, including billeting arrangements for civilian and service personnel, prior to and on the outbreak of war was to be carried out by all the departments concerned on a co-ordinated basis in accordance with the general plans framed in advance. Secondly, the Office of Works was to be responsible for the co-ordination of requisitioning. Thirdly, the Office of Works would assemble an inter-departmental committee to prepare co-ordinated plans. Fourthly, the arrangements decided upon would be notified to all government departments through a Treasury circular.

By November 1938, the register of earmarked properties was still in a very incomplete state. A number of departments had not yet transmitted lists of their full requirements, and the local authorities had not yet been notified at all. Munich revealed that there was considerable overlapping of demands for particular premises, which the whole exercise had been devised to prevent in the first place, thanks to imprecise addresses and inadequate descriptions of buildings. This was because much of the information had been produced in haste at short notice. Had the programme been put into practice in the autumn of 1938 the result would have been chaotic, and E.N. de Normann therefore set to work to improve the plan as far as possible in the breathing space acquired.

On 1 December 1938, he held a meeting with the representatives of the service departments in order to clarify their needs. They were advised to avoid requisitioning the property of local authorities such as town halls and swimming baths; hospitals, which would come under the control of the Ministry of

Health; cold stores, which would come under the Department of Food, Defence Plans; and railway, port and canal warehouses which would come under the aegis of the Ministry of Transport in the case of emergency.

The armed services were told to focus their requisitioning aims on private buildings. In practice, this restricted their field largely to country houses, of which they were to take the lion's share once war broke out. In January 1939, the War Office was given precedence for its training units above all other types of requisitioning. Though the Office of Works was responsible for the co-ordination, the actual requisitioning for military purposes was to be carried out directly by the War Office through regimental quartering commandants. The demands of the military were further concentrated on country houses by a War Office agreement to steer clear of commercial buildings such as Woolworth's stores, for instance, which would involve heavy expenditure on compensation for loss of trade.

At a meeting in de Normann's room at the Office of Works on 13 February 1939, it was decided to divide the central register into two portions: one covering Scotland to be kept in Edinburgh; and the other covering England, Wales and Northern Ireland, to be kept in London. It was emphasised that the register should continue to be treated as a secret document, so as to conceal the British government's war plans from enemy intelligence. Chief constables and the clerks to county councils were, however, to be informed of its contents. Copies of the stand-by register were to be kept ready in envelopes to send to liaison officers and regional commissioners in case of crisis, so as to minimise any delays in communication between central government and local representatives when the moment came.

The informal arrangements agreed with the service departments in December 1938 were clarified in the early months of 1939 by the institution of exempted categories of buildings which would not be available for requisitioning when war broke out. These were:

Government buildings and Local Authority buildings.
Premises owned by the Railways, Port Authorities, Canal Companies and Public Utilities.
Food warehouses and cold storage plant.
Hospitals.
Private dwelling houses with less than four rooms on the ground floor.

Industrial and commercial buildings were not formally declared to be exempt, but the compensation for loss of trading made it unlikely that they would be taken over for military purposes or billeting. Local Authorities were instructed to concentrate on garages, drill and village halls for ARP objectives and not to occupy country houses, which were to be restricted largely for the use of the military and evacuees, whether urban children, art treasures or hospital patients. Country houses were perfectly adapted to these plans both in scale and geography, many of them containing large-scale accommodation and being distributed evenly throughout the country with easy access by road and by rail from all urban centres.

Teams of local representatives from the Office of Works were divided into thirteen regional groups charged with discreetly surveying the buildings to be allotted to various government departments. The regional divisions comprised the north-east; the north-west; the north midlands; the Midlands, the south; the east; the west; the south-west; the south-east; London; Scotland; Wales; and Northern Ireland, the Isle of Man, Channel Isles and Scilly Isles.

The big question facing the officials was whether to tell the owners that their houses were being earmarked for requisitioning. Some local representatives did let the cat out of the bag. The result was 'a considerable volume of protest', with the risk of disclosure of the government's war plans to the enemy. The general feeling in the civil service was that private owners should not be told. The relevant minute reads that 'generally it seems desirable *not* to disclose the probability of requisitioning.'

While the owners themselves were not to be informed, the Office of Works agreed to circulate the relevant sections of the requisitioning register in the summer of 1939 to all the Local Authorities concerned. Some general guidelines were issued at the same time in response to requests from regional representatives as to how they should answer owners who might ask embarrassingly direct questions. Such people were to be told merely that 'a reconnaissance had been carried out in the area and that among other houses the one under discussion had naturally been considered, but that it was not possible to forecast what provision would be necessary if war breaks out'. Owners were to be assured, however, that compensation would be paid for any requisitioned property 'on a basis which will be determined hereafter by

Parliament'. In cases where the owners had actually offered their property to the government for use in case of war, they were to be told outright whether or not it would be accepted.

Several landowners were keen to make their houses, or rather buildings, available to the government for use in case of emergency out of a sense of public duty and patriotism. During the First World War many large houses had been used as hospitals and convalescent homes for troops, and *Country Life* had run a series of articles on 'What the Country Gentleman has Done for the War'. This traditional public-spirited attitude still coloured the outlook of many owners of country houses, especially the upper echelons of the peerage, at the outbreak of the Second World War. The Marquess of Salisbury, for instance, offered Hatfield as a military hospital just as he had done during the First World War; and the Earl of Harewood did likewise with Harewood. There was also a feeling that an owner might have more control over the fate of his house if he offered it for a particular purpose and laid down his own conditions, rather than waiting to have something imposed on him by government decree. Thus the Duke of Devonshire offered Chatsworth for use as a girls' school in the hope that this would provide the least damaging type of occupation for a building of major architectural importance containing an outstanding art collection. The Duke is reputed to have said, 'If there are young girls in the house, the authorities won't allow soldiers anywhere near the place.'

The wartime use of many country houses was decided in the event as much by acquaintance and connection, through family friends or relations, as by civil service diktat. The Duke of Bedford, for instance, offered Woburn Abbey to the hush-hush Imperial Intelligence Committee because his cousin, Captain the Hon. Leo Russell, worked in that department and had already sounded him out on the possibility of moving to Woburn when war broke out. Prep and public schools, in the cases where they moved, naturally tended to consider houses owned by old pupils or school governors. A large proportion of owners, however, especially of medium-sized country houses, made no plans of their own and did not envisage that their premises would be requisitioned. When notice was served on them in 1939 and 1940, it came as a considerable shock. They found themselves with very little time to pack up valuable collections of works of art, or to carry out protection work to fragile decorations and architectural features.

E.N. de Normann at the Office of Works was pleased with the way that the central register for requisition worked once the war had begun. On the whole it fulfilled its purpose in avoiding duplication and overlapping of demands, or unnecessary squabbling between different departments, and the Office of Works continued to keep the register up to date with additional earmarkings and revisions until it was closed on 15 December 1945, after the ending of hostilities. A survey of the working of the register in the winter of 1940/41 proved, however, that many of the original earmarkings had been well off target. A comparison of different departments showed that while the Admiralty had earmarked 2,800 premises and requisitioned the same number, the Air Ministry had earmarked only 5,000 but occupied 20,000. The civilian departments, on the other hand, earmarked more than they needed. The Board of Education ear-marked 4,000 premises but occupied only 3,000; the Ministry of Health earmarked 30,000 premises but took over only 18,500. As a result, many buildings were transferred between departments, and the War Office took over houses which in the first place had been reserved for other uses.

The register of earmarked properties continued to be kept confidential after the outbreak of war in September 1939, even though it was admitted within the civil service that, now that requisitioning was being put into operation, there was less need for strict secrecy. The original reason had been to protect the government's plans for evacuation from general knowledge. In the event, the regis-ter was kept secret throughout the war and until 1972. Civil servants are naturally secretive. As a result, in the early years of the war landowners were often alarmed by the unannounced arrival of a party of officials to survey their property for some mysterious purpose. In October 1942, Lord Ilchester came across an uninvited group of 'ministry officials' walking round his house, Melbury Park in Dorset, 'measuring it up for a possible hospital. He had no warning of their visit,' nor any prior hint of a requisition order. He raised the matter in the House of Lords the following month, but without any positive response. The first notice that Field Marshal Montgomery-Massingberd had that the Air Ministry intended to take over his estate at Gunby in Lincolnshire for an airfield was when he came across a man in the park marking the ancient oak trees. He asked him what he was doing and was told that they were to be felled for a runway! He went straight back to the house and rang the King to complain. It was only by campaigning vigorously at the highest levels and transferring the house to the National Trust that he was able to save the estate, which had belonged to the Massingberds since the Middle Ages, from total destruction.

Requisitioned property was taken on behalf of the Crown under the exercise of emergency powers – by order in council – according to Defence Regulation 51. The British government was, and still is, enabled to requisition property for emergency defence purposes under the Defence Act, 1842. Compensation for requisitioned property and land in the Second World War was paid according to guidelines laid down by Parliament in 1939 in the Compensation Defence Act 2 and 3 Geo.6 (see Appendix). Such payments were fixed as a 'sum equal to the rent which might reasonably be expected to be payable by a tenant . . . [but] no account shall be taken of any diminution or depreciation in value ascribable only to loss of pleasure or amenity'. The rents paid for properties varied. For Bletchley Park in Buckinghamshire, which was taken over as the Government Communications Headquarters on 1 June 1941, a rent of £150 per annum was paid to the owner, Mr Herbert Faulkener. The Red House, Bodicote, Oxfordshire, where the estate was taken over on 27 October 1944 for a Prisoner of War Programme, earned its owner a rent of £190 per annum, plus an extra £8 per annum for the kitchen garden. The scale of the rent depended on the size of the house and the number of outbuildings occupied. Thus at Roughwood Park, Buckinghamshire, the Davenport family received £400 per annum from 1942 to 1946 for the house, grounds, cottages and entrance lodges, while at Denham Lodge the Inland Revenue paid only £82.10s.0d. per annum during the period they occupied it as offices from 1941 to 1947. Those who gave their houses of their own accord at the beginning of the war often did not charge a rent. The Duke of Bedford and the Marquess of Salisbury, for instance, made Woburn and Hatfield available rent free for the duration of hostilities.

The concept of special architectural or historic interest played no part in the authorities' plans for requisitioning buildings in the war. Indeed, at that time, it would have been surprising if it had. Nearly the whole of the modern machinery for the protection of historic buildings in Britain has been built up since the Second World War, and was partly inspired by the destruction caused at that time. In 1939 there were no statutory lists of buildings of special architectural or historic interest, nor any other official means of taking such concepts into account in government policy. The owners themselves, of course, often knew and prized the history and artistic value of their houses and collections, but the whole requisitioning programme was evolved by civil servants and service chiefs on a confidential basis without consulting the owners. Any attempts to protect objects of architectural or artistic importance were left entirely in the hands of individual owners to negotiate as best they could when the time came. At Woburn, for instance, the Duke of Bedford and his land agent successfully insisted on a smoking restriction throughout the premises because the buildings were of historic interest and contained valuable art collections. It was at Lady Berwick's personal instigation that the delicate neo-classical decorations and marble chimneypieces at Attingham were boarded over by the Office of Works to protect them from the WAAFs who occupied the house.

The Office of Works was responsible for adapting many of the requisitioned buildings to their new use, providing materials for blackout, and for equipping them appropriately. Sometimes at the owner's insistence they carried out some protection work of special architectural features, such as boxing in carved woodwork or painted decorations. In general, more effort was made to protect the older, antiquarian houses than Georgian or Victorian ones. At Audley End, for instance, the Office of Works protected all the panelling with temporary boarding and even covered over the treads of the staircase to save them from accidental damage. At Parham Park in Sussex the Chief Inspector of Ancient Monuments was consulted on protection works. There was, however, no overall policy for protecting historic interiors while they were occupied by troops and evacuees. A great deal of damage could have been avoided if there had been. Gentlemen's agreements between officials and private owners at the beginning of the war did not last as long as the hostilities. Many houses were occupied successively by a number of different bodies, and the treatment of buildings tended to get rougher as the war continued and official attitudes became less gentlemanly.

The plan for requisitioning country houses formed only part of a wider programme for the compulsory acquisition by various government departments of a large range of buildings including hotels, parish halls, schools, institutions and even film studios★ for specific purposes. Nevertheless the wartime occupation of the country house can be seen in retrospect to mark a dramatic watershed in its evolution. Traditional country life had continued throughout the 1920s and 1930s still very much along Victorian lines, despite the poor profitability of agriculture in that period, and in spite of the late nineteenth-century eclipse of the unique political importance of the landed interest. The Second World War, however, changed all that. Compulsory requisitioning, combined with the socialist and corporatist ideals which the war effort helped to foster, contributed to a clean break. Those owners who returned to their houses after the war were able to replan them almost from scratch and to adapt to changed circumstances in a way that might not have been possible had it not been for the upheaval caused by requisitioning. As the young Duke of Bedford recorded when he returned to Woburn Abbey in 1955, there was nobody around to tell him what it was like in his grandfather's time. He was able to reorganise the house to suit himself, making a comfortable self-contained family home in the south wing with all modern conveniences and a 'small staff' of eleven indoor servants, and to rearrange the state rooms to display the eighteenth-century collections to the best advantage while throwing out a lot of

★ Pinewood Studios, for example, were requisitioned by the Ministry of Information.

Victorian clutter. He was then able to open the place to the public on a commercial scale and succeeded in turning an expensive dinosaur into a profitable business. Woburn is typical of what happened to many homes after the war, and such a radical break with tradition was made possible by the dramatic hiatus of wartime occupation.

Chapter II
Evacuees

"What I 'ates about this evacuation is the country makes the kids' voices sound so 'ollow."

It was generally assumed in the 1930s that London and the big provincial cities would be destroyed by aerial bombardment immediately on the declaration of war. In an article written in 1938, Winston Churchill stated, 'The prime factor of uncertainty in the world today is the menace from the air,' and many people in the years before the war speculated about that menace. Alexander Korda's 1936 film, *War of the Worlds*, based on a futuristic novel by H.G. Wells, presented a chilling picture of the effects of bombing from the air, with the destruction of London and the collapse of modern civilisation. The bombing scenes in the film were very convincing and, it was thought, prophetic of what was to come. The government warned repeatedly that the civilian populations in the cities would be in far greater danger in the coming war than in the First World War. Gas was expected, though in the event it never materialised, as well as heavy bombardment. Such air defences as existed seemed hopelessly inadequate. 'The bomber,' Stanley Baldwin pessimistically observed, 'will always get through.' In March 1938, Harold Nicolson recorded in his diary a speech by Malcolm MacDonald, then Colonial Secretary and a member of the Cabinet:

Malcolm says we are not strong enough to risk a war. It would mean the massacre of women and children in the streets of London. No government could possibly risk war when our anti-aircraft defences are in so farcical a condition.

The Anderson committee was set up in 1937 by the Home Office to look into the possibility of evacuating vulnerable civilians on the outbreak of war. It recommended that plans should be prepared for the total evacuation of certain classes of the population from the most densely congested urban and industrial areas to suitable houses in the country, and the Ministry of Health was made responsible for co-ordinating their billeting. In the plans that were drawn up, the principal groups chosen for evacuation were children, schools, institutions, orphanages, Barnardo Homes and working-class families from the East End of London and the big industrial cities. Immediately on the outbreak of war, these plans were put into action and those urban groups which had been designated were rapidly moved to 'safe' rural areas.

Rather to everybody's surprise, London was not immediately bombed on the outbreak of war. Conrad Russell, a cousin of the Duke of Bedford and friend of many literary figures, wrote to Lady Diana Cooper on 13 September 1939:

So far the greatest relief of this war has been the non-bombing. I had always pictured Hitler would begin the war by blowing London to smithereens and I thought he would do this as a surprise without warning and before there was time to evacuate people so that there would be panic, starvation, rioting and looting shops. Of course London might still be badly bombed but the surprise and dislocation of life couldn't occur now.

The evacuation of urban children at the beginning of the war went smoothly. They were dispersed from the cities by train, often in little groups with their names and destinations written on cardboard tags and tied to them, like pieces of luggage. At the other end of their journey they were collected and looked after by volunteer helpers, and divided up among earmarked premises. Many of the evacuees were lonely, homesick and pined in the country, away from the rough sociability of the crowded urban streets they were used to. There were great social difficulties on both sides in the sudden transfer from slum to country house. Evelyn Waugh, in his novel *Put Out More Flags*, describes the initial impact of a party of evacuee mothers and children from Birmingham billeted in the imaginary country house of Malfrey. The mothers spent their days queuing outside the village pub waiting for opening time and resented the attempts of Malfrey's chatelaine, Barbara Sothill, to be gracious to them:

When she left the chief mother said, 'What's she? Some kind of inspector I suppose, with her airs and graces. The idea of inviting us into the park. You'd think the place belonged to her the way she goes on.'

Though fiction, *Put Out More Flags* gives an accurate and evocative impression of the atmosphere of a large country house inhabited by urban evacuees, with a dwindling domestic staff, the main rooms closed up, and the central heating turned off to economise on fuel in the winter of 1939/40:

> The leaves fell in the avenue at Malfrey, and this year, where once there had been a dozen men to sweep them, there were only four and two boys . . . The Grinling Gibbons Saloon and the drawing rooms and galleries round it were shut up and shut off, carpets rolled, furniture sheeted, chandeliers bagged, windows shuttered and barred, hall and staircase stood empty and dark. Barbara lived in the little octagonal parlour which opened on the parterre, she moved the nursery over to the bedroom next to hers; what had once been known as the 'bachelors' wing' in the Victorian days when bachelors were hardy fellows who could put up with collegiate and barrack simplicity, was given over to the evacuees . . . the pipes were never heated and the chill in the house instead of being a mere negation of warmth became something positive and overwhelming . . .

Barbara's relations varied in their response to the evacuees. Her mother, Lady Seal, was frankly appalled:

> 'Poor Barbara has evacuees at Malfrey. What a shocking business! Dear dreaming Malfrey. Think of a Birmingham Board School in that exquisite Grinling Gibbons Saloon.'

Her brother Basil Seal, on the other hand, saw the evacuees as a potential source of income and, posing as a billeting officer, he used a particularly nauseating and incontinent family, the Connolly children, to terrorise the neighbours with nice houses into paying him sums of money not to have them billeted with them.

Nor must it be assumed that Waugh was exaggerating: he was writing from first-hand experience. His wife's family, the Herberts, had evacuees billeted on them at their country house, Pixton Park near Dulverton in Somerset, all through the Second World War and they left the house 'very knocked about' when they returned to their own homes. At Pixton on 1 October 1939, Waugh

> found a household of fifty-four, including twenty-six evacuated children, six spinster 'helpers', and most unexpectedly, a neighbouring doctor and his wife; he had been struck by a mortal disease and brought here to die. He was dying with unconscionable prolixity in the dining room. We ate (and helpers) in the hall, making a fine target for the children's spittle from the top landing . . . Mild flu and heavy colds raging.

Some at least of the children who were suddenly dumped on the hapless country house owner were almost totally unhouse-trained. James Money, who lived at the beginning of the war in an area of Kent near Tunbridge Wells designated as an area for evacuees from London, was personally involved in dealing with them and recalls various horror stories.

In September 1939 he spent the end of his long vacation from King's College, Cambridge, helping to cope with the trainloads of children descending from

London. He drove a car for the local evacuee organisation, picking up mothers and bewildered children at Tunbridge Wells station and transporting them in groups, first to the disinfestation centre and then to their new homes. He recalls that as dissimilar social groups which had never before come into contact were forcibly thrown together, evacuee stories began to circulate thick and fast, the chief purveyors and editors of these astonishing tales being the Women's Voluntary Service (WVS) and Air Raid Precautions (ARP).

> There was, for instance, the case of old Lady C— who, having failed in her efforts to enthuse the evacuee children with Victorian animal books, faded photographs of her youth and collections of wild flowers, finding that they were not interested in the herbaceous part of her garden and had consumed all her fruit in the first week of their stay, in desperation organised them into a game of hunt-the-thimble on her richly carpeted drawing room floor and so caused them to adopt the position which their mothers had taught them for quite another purpose . . .

A house near Matfield was unfortunate enough to be allotted six East End boys of 'extreme wickedness', who confined their owners to the servants' hall and then proceeded to rearrange and redecorate the main part of the house as a new and sumptuous version of gang headquarters in London. The walls were stripped of their homely watercolours and covered with obscene murals in paint and soot. Only the intervention of the local constabulary saved the distressed owners from a complete breakdown.

Yet another reluctant hostess was surprised to discover 'the seat of the downstairs WC missing from its moorings and more than ever bewildered to find it some days later hanging on the wall of the bedroom occupied by an evacuee mother, who had used it to frame a photograph of her absent husband'.

Each of the big provincial cities, like London, evacuated into their hinterland. Manchester sent children to Cheshire; the industrial north-east to Cumberland and Northumberland; Bristol to Somerset. Thus evacuee stories became a nationwide phenomenon and were no doubt suitably embellished and exaggerated as time passed, though the unadorned reality could be depressing enough.

Conrad Russell wrote laconically from Mells in Somerset, where over two hundred 'refugees' were billeted in the neighbourhood, to Lady Diana Cooper on 4 October 1939:

Today I saw Lady Weymouth. She has thirty-four *extra* people in her not very big house. They are crippled children – they are very dirty and the nurses who attend them are dirty too, so the whole house is smelly.

Institutions like orphanages were often better disciplined and their children more under control than those of individual families. Barnardo Homes, which occupied several houses during the war including Chawton House in Hampshire and Lilleshall in Staffordshire, were run on very strict lines; any boy who ran away, for instance, was threatened with the rather excessive punishment of fifteen strokes of the cane. Nor were all evacuated children by any means rowdy and incontinent, though they could be hard work in houses with drastically reduced domestic staff and elderly owners not used to dealing with children. At Lyme Park in Cheshire, forty evacuated children from Manchester happily occupied the house throughout the war without impinging on the owner, Lord Newton, who lived mainly in the library with a roaring log fire and a lot of dogs.

Many evacuees did not stay in the country for the whole six years of war. Several returned to London as soon as the worst of the Blitz was over. There was, in any case, an official policy in the summer of 1942 to return as many children as possible to their own homes in order to free country houses to provide the accommodation needed for the American troops pouring into England for the Second Front.

At the other extreme of the social hierarchy from slum children, plans were formulated for the evacuation of the royal family in case of emergency. Pitchford Hall in Shropshire, the picturesque black and white, half-timbered, sixteenth-century, E-shaped house of the Grant family was chosen as a refuge for Princess Elizabeth and Princess Margaret in the event of an invasion. As the house lies in the hollow of a narrow valley, aeroplanes could not see it from the air and it was therefore deemed especially safe; to protect it further it was referred to in official documents as 'Code X'. It never proved necessary to put this particular evacuation plan into action, and King George VI, Queen Elizabeth and the two princesses spent most of the war at Windsor Castle which, being a medieval fortress, was considered strong enough to offer protection from aerial bombardment. The royal family also continued to go to Sandringham from time to time. For this reason, the interior of Appleton Hall, a subsidiary house on the estate originally built for Princess Maud, one of Queen Victoria's daughters, was converted into immensely strong air raid shelters. So substantial were these constructions that the cost of their removal after the war was judged prohibitive, and as a result the house has been empty and derelict ever since.

The government insisted, however, that the widow of George V, Queen Mary, should leave Marlborough House in London and stay in a secret hide-out in the country for the duration of the war, in order not to add to their immediate responsibilities. Had the decision been left to her she would have preferred to stay in London, her home. Badminton in Gloucestershire, the seat of the Duke of Beaufort, was chosen because the Duchess (a daughter of the Duke of Cambridge) was Queen Mary's niece. For the whole six years that Queen Mary spent at Badminton, no mention was made of her retreat by the government or in the press in case the attention of the enemy should be drawn to it. The Queen liked Badminton and remarked, 'I've adopted the house and family as my own.' The Beauforts dealt with a potentially difficult situation with tact and humour, relishing such moments as Queen Mary handing a Spratts biscuit to the Bishop of Gloucester, saying, 'Give that to the little dog', and the poor man, being deaf, thought it was for him and 'munched it up'.

There was a trial run in September 1938 at the time of Munich when the government suggested that the Queen should go down to Badminton to inspect the house to see whether it would suit her as a retreat should war come. Osbert Sitwell, a cousin of the Beauforts, was staying in the house at the same time and accompanied her on several strenuous sightseeing tours to Bath and its vicinity. He recorded one particular incident when they passed a large institutional building on their way home from Bath. The Queen said,

> 'How interesting! That must be the School for the Orphan Daughters of Officers that my mother used to take such an interest in!' At that moment the children began to converge on the road; they were carrying hockey-sticks, and stared in a desultory, adenoidal kind of way at the large royal motor and its august occupant, who on this occasion, as usual, sat just behind the driver in a small upright seat, so that she was very visible. As Queen Mary passed the girls, she waved her hand and smiled at them, but they merely stood still, mooning at Her Majesty vacantly, and then I heard Queen Mary observe to herself, '*Cheer*, little idiots, can't you?'

In September 1939 the Queen descended on Badminton with enormous quantities of luggage and a vast retinue. The Duchess of Beaufort told James Pope-Hennessy at the time he was writing Queen Mary's biography of her reaction when she saw Her Majesty arrive: 'I was scared stiff – more than fifty of them descended on me one afternoon and I was alone; Master was away. You've never seen anything like that arrival in your life.' As well as the cohorts of the royal attendants, there were some seventy pieces of luggage. The servants who were evacuated with the Queen were difficult, and carped and grumbled from the start. They missed their domestic life in London or in cosy cottages at Sandringham.

The rather singular basic arrangement made was that Her Majesty should take the house as a whole for the war years, except for two bedrooms and a sitting room which the Beauforts were allowed to retain for their own use. They were to stay on, with their own servants, but rather as if they were guests in their own home; they had their meals at her table. Though the Beauforts were fond of Queen Mary and revered her, they found this 'system of dyarchy' a great strain. The Queen rapidly took over and arranged both her own life and everybody else's. The dowager, Louisa Duchess of Beaufort, who lived in The Cottage in the village was perhaps more put out than her son and daughter-in-law. Used to being the chief old lady of the region she was dismayed to find herself 'outshone by a much bigger setting sun'.

Queen Mary herself was blithely unaware of these background tremors. Her own formal world still revolved around her, with familiar courtiers and servants in attendance. The eighteenth-century architecture of the house with its grandly ducal façade and enfilades of portrait-hung rooms gave off the air of an eighteenth-century court, perhaps the *Residenz* of a German baroque prince. The Queen used the dining room with its Grinling Gibbons carvings as her drawing room and the Oak Room with dark sixteenth-century panelling from Raglan Castle as her dining room. Upstairs she had her own suite comprising a bedroom, with silk upholstered four-poster, private sitting room and bathroom.

At first, the Queen continued with her favourite

hobby of sightseeing, making exhausting forays to picturesque old buildings in the neighbourhood. But soon jaunts of this type became impossible because of petrol rationing and so Queen Mary occupied herself with war work: collecting scrap iron (including farm implements left in the fields which all had to be returned to their owners); sorting and annotating the Beaufort family archives in the Muniment Room; and forestry work or 'wooding' on the estate, which provided winter firewood for companies of soldiers billeted nearby. In order to supervise work in the woods she had herself drawn to the site by horses, sitting in a bath chair on a farm cart, to save petrol. The Duchess said, 'You look as if you were in a tumbril, Aunt May.' 'Well it may come to that yet; one never knows,' was the reply. She would go out in all weathers from two to five every afternoon. Her entourage loathed it; Lady Cynthia Colville lost her wedding ring and Major Wickham broke his wrist. Two chauffeurs were knocked out by it and another damaged an eye and had to wear a black patch. They would all dodge behind the undergrowth to read and smoke like truant schoolboys till she caught them and dragged them back to chopping trees, clearing brambles or stripping ivy. The Queen supervised in person, jabbing at recalcitrant branches with her walking stick.

She tried to cut down a magnificent cedar tree on the south lawn at Badminton, but the Duke drew the line at that and refused point blank to allow it. The tussle continued for several years, but the tree survived, and is still standing. The Duke was particularly anxious to preserve it because of the family tradition that Lord Raglan, of Crimean War fame, had played in it as a small boy.

The courtiers found rustic life, with everybody talking about hunting and hay-making not entirely to their liking. Maggie Wyndham complained about the lack of intellectual conversation at Badminton. She wanted to discuss Italy and Trollope and paintings, not horses, farming and dogs. Queen Mary, on the other hand, though totally urban, got used to the country: 'Oh *that's* what hay looks like, is it? I never knew that.'

Both the courtiers and the Beauforts suffered alike from the meagre helpings of food at meals. Queen Mary constantly fussed about keeping strictly to rations. She cut herself, and them, down to the minimum, while the servants lived on the fat of the land beyond the green baize door. The Queen wished to set an example and not to have people saying that she benefited from special treatment. At the end of a hard day's work, there would be one small partridge for dinner for six people or half a little snipe each. Dinner was at eight-thirty prompt every night and, despite the scanty food, was a formal occasion. Queen Mary would dress in a sequined gown, ostrich-feather cape and several rows of pearls.

As well as the strict enforcement of food rationing, other notes of austerity were introduced. Instead of fresh table linen, a washable oil cloth designed to look like white damask was used, and the napkins were made to last a week, everybody keeping their own in a ring as if at school. Queen Mary had a heavy silver ring engraved with a crown and her monogram. Dinner lasted for only half an hour and at nine o'clock they switched on the wireless to hear the news every night. Luncheon often comprised 'Lord Woolton pie', a vegetarian concoction nicknamed after the Minister for Food.

The Queen was frightened of being kidnapped by the Nazis. Arrangements were made for taking her away by plane to a secret destination if the Germans landed. She always had three suitcases packed ready in case of trouble. Her Majesty kept one, and the other two were handed over to two dressers, one for each of them to guard. If an alert was given of an air raid it was also their duty to pack a fourth suitcase with jewels and tiaras. During air raids the lady-in-waiting took this case down to the shelter made in the reinforced cellar.

The bombing of Bath and Bristol, only a few miles away, brought Badminton close to the war and, when the alert was sounded, the Queen would descend to the shelter. The Duchess of Beaufort told James Pope-Hennessy of her disconcerting experience on the earliest of these occasions. During the first air raid, a message was sent to the Duchess that Queen Mary was in the reinforced shelter and wished her to come down.

It was a mistake, of course; she hadn't sent for me at all. Well, there I was in the middle of the night, with my hair all anyhow and in a filthy old dressing gown; and there in the shelter sat Queen Mary, perfectly dressed with her pearls, doing a crossword puzzle. On one side of her was her lady [Constance Milnes-Gaskell], who had taken a sleeping pill and kept sagging over to one side. Whenever the Queen said, 'High Life in six letters beginning with a T, Constance,' she'd just grunt 'huh-huh-huh', and flop over again; on the other side of the Queen was her maid, gripping two jewel cases grimly; I never did that again, I just couldn't compete.

The air raids brought a further royal evacuee to Badminton in the shape of the splendid Rysbrack bronze equestrian statue of King William III from Queen Square in Bristol. It was moved to Badminton after the first bombing, at Queen Mary's invitation, and temporarily rested on the lawn in front of the house facing down the Long Avenue towards the distant Worcester Lodge.

Osbert Sitwell, who was invited to Badminton on several occasions during the war, in order to help his cousins entertain the Queen, has left a series of vivid vignettes which capture precisely the atmosphere of this great ducal house in wartime. On his first visit in January 1941, Queen Mary had already been in residence for fifteen months:

I had never seen the house look finer, perhaps because after a period of some years when certain rooms were not much used, now again it appeared as if the whole extent of it were lived in. It had always, moreover, preserved a peculiar air of the past, because things had been left alone, and objects left where they were. Thus in the hall, the white light radiating from the thin and scintillant layer of frost outside played on the dry white Italian plasterwork, on the dark frescos by Richard Wooton depicting the sports of the first Duke, and sparkled on the silver tops of the maces, which carried by footmen in the time of Queen Anne, still stood in a corner near the fireplace. Though an air of extra prosperity and polish now prevailed, the rooms in general were untouched, nothing had been moved: the only visible change consisted in the presence of a guard outside the house, which added to the atmosphere a suggestion that its occupants might be prisoners, and thereby induced a distant sense of gloom or doom.

Sitwell's final visit to Badminton during Her Majesty's occupation of the house was at Christmas 1944 when he formed part of a house party which included the Beauforts, the Earl of Harewood, the Princess Royal, Lord Claud Hamilton, Sir Richard Molyneux and the ladies-in-waiting. Servants were numerous, if aged. The main change was that, much to their chagrin, they now wore blue battledress with the royal cypher (designed by George VI) rather than the old royal livery of scarlet and gold. All the paraphernalia of a Victorian royal Christmas was much in evidence. In the hall glittered a large lighted Christmas tree, and there was a long table covered with a purple cloth on which was displayed an array of Christmas presents. To find appropriate gifts for so many people in wartime was not easy, and the Beauforts and Sitwell resorted to a subterfuge. They agreed to 'give' him something which he had already bought for himself, and they would choose something from the lumber room for him to 'give' to them. So he received a hundred Turkish cigarettes, and they got a book and an eighteenth-century green shagreen étui. This rather back-fired as Queen Mary, with her keen interest in *objets d'art*, was fascinated by the étui and wanted to know where he had acquired it!

On Christmas Eve and Christmas Day the whole party attended service in the eighteenth-century church which is joined on to the side of the house like a private chapel; a log fire burned in the fireplace in the family pew. Several local grandees turned up for dinner on Christmas Day, including an officer with the title of Captain of the Garrison. The food was good, if exiguous, and champagne was served. Queen Mary wore cloth of silver, huge sapphires, a pearl collar and enormous diamond pendants and brooches. Osbert Sitwell recalled, 'As this magnificent figure, blazing and sparkling, led the way from the room, Dick Molyneux turned to me and said in his loud, deaf voice, like that of a man shouting from a cave into a strong wind, "I wonder if you realise it, but after that old lady has gone, you'll never see anything like this, or like her, again!" '

Queen Mary left Badminton for London on 11 June 1945. The Duchess of Beaufort wrote on 18 May:

The Queen is here until 11th June. I expect it is Marlborough House that is in a state of eruption, revolt and tumult. Vans of boxes and hampers and trunks all marked with the royal cypher continually leave the house. Today I saw such a van leaving with royal crowns and MRs bursting from every side, but at the very back and perched on top of these dignified boxes sat, very cheerily and cheekily a common enamel slop-pail – very plebeian, and showing no sign of its royal ownership.

Chapter III
Schools

Of all the different uses to which country houses were put during the Second World War, occupation by schools is the best remembered. Intelligent children who spent several years in a building of great architectural interest surrounded by beautiful landscape were often profoundly affected by the experience and have remembered it in vivid detail for the rest of their lives. A whole range of schools was evacuated to country houses, including a nursery school in the case of Waddesden Manor in Buckinghamshire, though girls' boarding schools and boys' prep schools were among the most common migrants and the best remembered. Some state schools and boys' public schools also moved into country houses, but in fewer numbers. Not all of the schools which migrated to the country did so for reasons of their own safety, and many boarding schools in the west of Britain (which was beyond the range of German bombing raids from the beginning of the war till the fall of France) moved because their own buildings were requisitioned by various government departments for offices, thus making it necessary for them to find new quarters elsewhere.

War broke out at the end of the school holidays, and on the whole children found it rather an exciting prospect. Many of those due to return to boarding school found their departure happily delayed. Instead of going back to school in the ordinary way, pupils received instructions to stay at home for a couple of weeks while arrangements were made for the occupation of alternative premises. Thus, when they belatedly set off to school, many pupils had no idea where they were going. The train took them to a specified destination. When they got off, there was a mysterious drive through uncharted country, till suddenly the bus turned in at a majestic lodge gate and traversed a seemingly endless gravel drive before halting in front of a gigantic and elaborate building which was from now on to be 'school'.

Mary Frazer, who was a pupil at Craigmount School in Edinburgh when war broke out, recalls what it felt like at the end of the summer holidays when they were all told to stay at home for a few extra days, and then, a fortnight after the original starting date of term, were told to go to Perth: 'More excitement! We were taken by train to Perth and then came a drive by bus out on the Blairgowrie road and through the main gate of Scone Palace. The thrill of that first glimpse through the ancient archway remains with me still.' Craigmount School remained at Scone throughout the war and for some years after, till 1952 when the Earl of Mansfield, whose house it was, moved back in and the school transferred to Minto House in Roxburghshire. After the constricted urban site in Edinburgh, the large policies and Regency Gothic buildings of Scone proved a welcome metamorphosis to Mary Frazer:

A lovelier and more historic spot than Scone Palace could hardly have been chosen. The extensive grounds . . . were beautiful, although neglected

during those difficult years. We could walk down
the fields to the Tay, skate on the curling pond and,
with permission, visit what remained of the Abbey
in the policies. We loved it. Life was so much freer
than it had been in the city.

From the point of view of the children the sudden
transfer of school to what seemed a palace in the
country was a thrilling excitement. To the owner,
however, it was often a traumatic shock when his
quiet country house suddenly became a replica of
St Trinians. Ralph Dutton, later Lord Sherborne,
recorded his feelings about the requisitioning as a
school of his own house, Hinton Ampner in Hampshire, which he had only just finished remodelling in
the Georgian taste when the war broke out. In the
summer of 1939, he received an official letter giving
him the choice of either accommodating forty children evacuated from London, or handing the whole
house over to the Portsmouth Day School for Girls
which was due to be moved out from the bombing
danger zone around the Royal Dock Yard. He chose
the school, and in due course a hundred camp
beds and other pieces of equipment arrived and
were stored in the cellars. In August, he went
away on holiday, and was shocked to receive a
telegram on the 29th saying that the school had
been ordered to Hinton forty-eight hours later. He
rushed home as fast as he could and started to
clear the rooms of their contents, moving the fine
Regency furniture into the stables and his collection
of porphyry objects and valuable paintings into the
library which was the one room on the ground
floor not to be occupied by the school so as to

avoid the necessity of moving the books from its shelves.

Punctually at ten o'clock on 1 September 1939, a fleet of buses drew up at the front door and out poured a crowd of little girls each carrying a small suitcase. They rushed shouting and laughing into the house. For Ralph Dutton

It was a moment of intense bitterness: just as many months of work and effort had reached their culmination, all was snatched from me. Nowadays one is more accustomed to the buffets of fortune, but in 1939 I found it difficult to comprehend that I was being turned out of my own house. However, the situation had to be accepted, and picking up my suitcase, I left.

Later, when he heard of the fate of houses in military occupation, he realised how fortunate he was to have his populated by little girls. Many owners deliberately plumped for girls' schools, if given the choice, as the gentlest users for a fragile old building. Several of the greatest historic houses became girls' schools for that reason, including, as well as Scone, Drumlanrig, Chatsworth, Longleat, Elton, Crichel, Duncombe, Knebworth, Longstowe and Castle Howard, though in the latter case with disastrous results, as it turned out. One of the advantages of having girls in the house was that many of the paintings, tapestries, pieces of sculpture and larger pieces of furniture could be left *in situ* without too great a risk; the girls could be positively good for 'the things', providing some warmth, the right degree of humidity and ventilation.

At Chatsworth, the Duke of Devonshire decided

on a girls' school as his wartime tenant as soon as the conflict became inevitable, and he offered the house to Penrhos College, a Welsh public school whose own buildings at Colwyn Bay on the North Wales coast were due to be commandeered by the Ministry of Food as offices. At first, knowledge of requisitioning was restricted to the headmistress and chairman of the governors and it was only on 7 September, zero day for the sentence of exile on the public schools, that the rest of the staff were informed and the arrangements for moving to Derbyshire put into force. The headmistress was apologetic to her colleagues, but explained that confirmation of the government's secret plans had only arrived in that morning's post and she was unable to divulge them before then. The staff were flabbergasted. One of them recalled:

There was a moment of stunned silence, followed by a positive babel of chatter. How and where did one start on such an upheaval? The first thing that leapt to the mind was Miss Smith's suggestion of some time off; we needed it now to gather ourselves together.

This breathing space was necessarily brief, and within twenty-four hours plans were beginning to emerge for the loading of the twenty to thirty lorries the Ministry intended to use. These vehicles would travel day and night between Colwyn Bay and Chatsworth with a view to accomplishing the entire move within a matter of ten days.

There were several battles to be fought. The Ministry saw no need for wardrobes and surely one chair per girl and a solitary piano would be enough? We eventually took twenty-two pianos

and an adequate number of chairs and wardrobes,
but there remained the vexed question of rain damage to goods travelling in open lorries. The thought
of soaked mattresses and bedding and of dripping
stationery was too much to bear; there might be
a war on, but even so some degree of common
sense was essential! At last the Ministry agreed to
provide a number of furniture vans, and the great
'pack up' got under way with a minimum of delay.

Meanwhile, the senior mistress set off to contact
the Duke and Duchess of Devonshire, and with them
prepare for Penrhos's arrival. It was a daunting under-
taking, for it was hard to visualise staff bedrooms and
dormitories, formrooms and dining halls in the vast
baroque and neo-classical rooms of Chatsworth. Yet
the co-operation and help which the school received
was warm and generous. Difficulties, as far as possible, were smoothed away as rooms were cleared and,
one by one, re-allocated to their new uses. The senior
mistress recalls:

> The names of the rooms themselves were
> fascinating: Yellow Silk Drawing Room, Green
> Satin, State Music Room, Red Velvet – all about
> to become either dormitories or formrooms; the
> squash court in the stables would make an adequate
> gymnasium, the laundry a domestic science depart-
> ment, and the orangery into which the Ministry
> lorries were unloading all the school's belongings
> would eventually provide an art room and space
> for lockers. Pianos would shortly nestle in odd
> corners under statues, the servants' and stewards'
> halls would be converted into dining rooms, but

these were likely to be crowded and an overflow of staff would consequently eat in the housemaids' pantry. The splendid Painted Hall would be ideal for prayers with the choir sitting up the soaring Great Staircase; the fully equipped small theatre would cater for plays and entertainments.

A vast amount of work was required at Chatsworth. Carpets, the best furniture and objects of art had to be moved from the rooms and stored in appropriate conditions. Chandeliers had to be bagged, four-poster beds (too big to move) protected by dust sheets, carved panelling and tapestries boarded over to prevent accidental damage. The contents removed from the state apartments and other rooms due to be occupied by the school were carefully stacked in the chapel, library and sculpture gallery. This mammoth task came on top of the work already in progress of dismantling and clearing up the remains of the celebrations for the coming of age of the Marquess of Hartington, the Duke's eldest son (killed in action in 1944) which had taken place in August 1939. The Chatsworth staff, with remarkable efficiency, accomplished everything in eleven days and with a great effort all was ready for the arrival of the Penrhos girls on 26 September, a glorious autumn day. Doreen North (née Douglas), the head girl at the time, has written down her first impressions of their arrival:

I will always remember driving along the winding road over Paine's Bridge and up to the main entrance with my trunk bumping in the boot of our car. Chatsworth looked magnificent on that autumn day. The stone was lit up with sunshine and the house smiled a glorious welcome. The warmth of the Devonshire family greeted the girls immediately for the Duke had asked for all the fountains to be turned on – even the Great Emperor Fountain raised itself to the sky. Could this really be a return to school? Everyone felt bemused. It was all quite enchanting and on we went through the avenue of tulip trees to the front door. It was all so luxurious and thrilling to be shown the bedroom for four of us in the White Satin Room. I loved it all.

Then we had a grand tour along countless corridors used as dormitories with rows and rows of beds and chests of drawers from Colwyn Bay. The state rooms were full of them – as also numerous smaller rooms like the Red Velvet and the Sabine Room.

The impact of the Painted Hall and the oak stairs was quite astounding – but what was that tiny hand-powered organ doing at the foot of the Great Staircase? Surely this wasn't to accompany our excellent choir singing all our beautiful anthems – but it was!

The girls were allowed to use almost every part of the house, and had complete freedom of the gardens, woods and park, though the villages of Edensor and Baslow were out of bounds. The 10th Duke, who had only inherited Chatsworth a short time before on the death of his father in 1938, moved back to a smaller house on the estate, Churchdale near Ashford-on-the-Water. But he and the Duchess and the Dowager Duchess, who also lived nearby, all

visited from time to time. Certain rules were impro-
vised to protect the house. Dustless chalk was used
on the blackboards, and sand was sprinkled on the
floors before sweeping. All school work was done in
pencil, only the sixth form being allowed the use of
ink. 'Running indoors was a real and punishable sin.'
Despite these precautions, some accidents did happen.
A group of fifth formers lit a small bonfire under the
thermometer outside the front door to test its efficacy
and all the mercury shot to the top and stuck there.
In one of the drawing rooms, a dose of Eno's was
splashed on to one of the paintings left hanging on
the wall, and a picture-restorer had to be summoned
hurriedly to deal with the results.

Francis Thompson, the elderly and erudite ducal
librarian, stayed on at Chatsworth throughout the
war. He did his best to interest the girls in the history
of the house and its treasures and put on little exhi-
bitions for them of books, manuscripts, gold snuff
boxes or similar selections from the collection, in the
glazed cases in the Grotto off the Painted Hall. He
encouraged them to ask questions about the house.
One little girl wanted to know how many windows
there were. 'They counted them hand in hand', and
found that there were 397 external windows. Another,
whose dormitory was a room the walls of which
were painted with the legend of the Rape of the
Sabine Women, asked him, 'Please, Mr Thompson,
what exactly is a rape?' The poor man lost his head
and referred her to the headmistress for details. At
first somewhat overawed by their surroundings, the
girls soon got used to them. 'We felt it wasn't everybody that went out for a walk and hobnobbed with
dowager duchesses.' One girl, when asked what she

thought about being at school amidst so many art treasures, replied, 'Oh, we're getting used to it, we hardly mind them at all now.'

Chatsworth is situated high up in the central hills of England and the winters are long and cold. The lack of heat and the rationing of food were the two main drawbacks of life there. But the school collected logs in the park and kept fires burning in the Chapel Corridor which served as a general meeting area and recreation room. Doreen North remembers:

The open fires were enticing and created a homely warmth we hadn't experienced in Colwyn Bay. We collected and roasted chestnuts, made toast on long forks and even grilled sausages in front of hot embers. One evening a group of fourth formers fancied baked beans, but, alas, didn't possess a tin opener so threw the tin into the fire to heat. There was an almighty explosion in the Chapel Corridor and beans were hurled in every direction – all over the beautiful stone fireplace and into the caique [in which the 6th Duke had sailed on the Bosphorus]. Fortunately, all was cleared up by hungry girls before a member of the Chatsworth staff came round to tend the fire again.

In the arctic Derbyshire winters, the numerous copies of classical statues which adorned the gardens at Chatsworth looked so cold in their marble nudity that the girls considerately bedecked them with scarves, bras, and woolly balaclavas.

Though remote, Chatsworth was not entirely isolated from the arena of war, especially when the Germans started to bomb Sheffield, only a few miles over the moors to the north. Doreen North recalls:

When the sirens went during the night, everyone had to go down to the cellars. Now we knew which staff had curl bobs – they looked so different in their dressing gowns and bed socks! It's funny, but I have no memory of feeling cold down there – but I must say I suffered from claustrophobia with the thought of the weight of Chatsworth overhead. I think this was the reason, no heroics, I suggested prefects should fire-watch on the roof. This was arranged, and stirrup pumps were provided and prefects practised, just in case. I remember being on duty up there when Sheffield was blitzed. The German bombers flew in on the upper side of Chatsworth and back on the riverside following the silver ribbon of river to Derby. The sky over Sheffield was a blaze of reddish gold from all the incendiary bombs. Next day we discovered the main shopping centre had suffered due to the inaccuracy of the German bombing which had been intended to annihilate the adjacent industrial buildings . . .

On another occasion a Wellington bomber crashed in the park.

Later during the war, Chatsworth itself came within an ace of being bombed. A couple of low-flying German planes mistook the River Derwent for the River Wye and thought the house must be the factory making batteries for submarines at Bakewell, recognised their mistake but machine gunned the building in pique. Several bedrooms had bullet-holes in their inside walls, but the girls were downstairs at the time and no one was hurt. The scars on the stonework are still visible on the north side of the house. Another time an American plane doing machine gun practice over the East Moor behind the house peppered that side of the building with bullets, one of which remains embedded in a library table to this day.

When the time came to leave Chatsworth, the girls felt homesick for the place and missed it. Doreen North spoke for many of her contemporaries when she said,

> I was very sad to leave Penrhos and Chatsworth and look back on the two years I spent there, realising it was an experience of a lifetime. I often remember the magnificent stately home set in a beautiful Derbyshire valley, romantic walks in the woodland, picnics by the 'blasted oaks', sunbathing in the Azalea Dell and swimming in the lake near the Hunting Tower.

The wartime arrangements at the other large country houses which became girls' schools were similar to those at Chatsworth. At Longleat, for example, when the Royal School was evacuated from Bath in 1940 in order that the Admiralty could occupy its own buildings, the state apartments were converted into staff rooms and dormitories. The Marquess of Bath, then an old man, continued, however, to live in a corner of the house alongside the school. He was a familiar, if distant, figure pottering around the house and garden with his ancient great dane, Stephen. He continued to live his own life regardless of the school's presence, entertaining his family and friends for Christmas and other traditional occasions.

Conrad Russell went over from Mells to Longleat for Christmas dinner in 1941 and noted, 'We had caviare – the gift of Aubrey Smith – turkey, plum pudding, mince pies and I ate all courses . . . we all ate to repletion. Lord B did yesterday's *Daily Mirror* CWP [cross word puzzle] quite solemnly' as they sat dozily round the fire afterwards.

The strongest memory of the school's pupils was of the cold in their part of the house during the first winter at Longleat. There was no heating in the state rooms, and the water in the washstand jugs in the dormitories used to freeze solid. The only fire was in the Great Hall, which was such an enormous room that the few glowing logs made scant impact on the chill. The girls were allowed to carry rugs and eiderdowns with them all the time in order to keep out the cold, and they hung their underclothes in the hot cupboard in the servery off the State Dining Room to thaw. Mrs Aylmer, who was at school at Longleat for four years during the war, remembers the experience well:

At the outbreak of war the Admiralty commandeered the premises of the Royal School at Lansdowne, Bath, as offices with a greater measure of safety than in London. Thereupon the Marquess of Bath offered to have the school at Longleat (very sensibly for fear of having something worse and causing dirt, damage or destruction – the RS girls were a very disciplined lot, à la mode in those days, and there was no toothpaste flicked on to the Chinese wallpapers or indeed any damage due to the school's occupation of Longleat, so far as I am aware).

A 'temporary' wooden four-sided classroom

block was erected parallel with the west front of the house, with a covered way leading to the basement side door, past what was then the chapel, which had death watch beetle and was not in use. The classrooms were built without foundations and raised in the form of a square with grass in the middle and a verandah passage around the inner side for access to the classrooms, gym, and two science labs (the sheep grazing in the park would come under the building for shade in summer, and give the place a pungent smell in consequence!). After dusk, when it was an offence to show any light, the girls were responsible by rota for putting up specially made shutters to conform with the black-out regulations. These made the heated classrooms extremely stuffy, in very marked contrast to the freezing cold and damp experienced in winter in the dormitories and indeed most of the rest of Longleat House.

I think I could go round Longleat now and remember which rooms were used for what forty-five years ago. Lord Bath had his suite of rooms on the south side, i.e. on the ground floor immediately to the left of the main front entrance. Next was the Gatehouse-sanatorium. The Great Hall the other side of the front entrance was used every day for prayers (c. seven-fifty am before breakfast and in the evening) and for assemblies, occasional concerts and play-acting and before going into meals. The Red Library on the east side of the house overlooking the terrace was one of the rooms used as dining rooms, but not the Green Library in the south-east corner, which was used to store furniture covered in dust sheets. The smallest or little dining room was 'French speaking', and there was a further one which must be in the north-east corner of the house with a servery adjoining. Beyond that were the back stairs, on the north side, they led down to the basement kitchens and up to the first and second floors. The food all came up by a hand-operated lift, it seemed antiquated even *c.* 1940, and if inexpertly used by pulling on the rope too hard, or applying the 'brake' too fast, the plates would land a floor below with a fearful clatter. The cleaning and servicing was done in part by very young and incompetent Irish maids, though the girls did a lot of table laying, clearing, serving, etc.

The headmistress's study and sitting room were in the north-west corner of Longleat, with bedroom and, I believe, secretary's office adjoining. The wide passage running along the inner west side still had all the showcases containing Sèvres china, etc. and this ground floor passage was in regular use, but the girls were strictly forbidden to run and were not given to rioting outside the head's rooms, so it came to no harm.

The girls were only allowed to use the back stairs and those leading down to the basement from the front hall, not the spiral stairs used by domestic staff (but must have done so to get up on to the flat roof to sunbathe and dry hair). Only teaching staff could use the main front stairs, and it was risky but tempting as a short cut to use them to reach the hall in time for prayers, only to run into the wrathful headmistress.

Almost all the first floor rooms were used as girls' dormitories, that is, all the west range with

Chinese wallpapers, those on the south front, the passage past the front stairs, the ballroom or long gallery and rooms over the dining room in the north-east corner; next to the adjoining servery was a housemistress's bed-sitting room and a small dispensary near the back stairs. Opposite these stairs and along the north side were more dormitories and several other staff bed-sitting rooms. The first floor room in the south-east corner and Bishop Ken's Library were full of furniture, but not kept locked, so one could occasionally slip in for a quiet read or to enjoy the rare luxury of being alone for a few moments. Domestic staff were accommodated on the floor above.

The cellars were the main route between the house and classrooms; they were used to store school trunks, etc., and also a large collection of hip baths relegated there from all over the house, and they were used to sort waste paper for recycling, and on at least one occasion as containers for elderberries, which were then picked off their stalks, stewed and served for supper (with disastrous results).

There were very few bathrooms, and girls were limited to one a week, with not more than five inches of water; there were several 'water holes' where large cans were filled morning and evening to carry water to the dormitories for washing in shared individual 'old-fashioned' china basins; the dirty water was then carried back in 'slop buckets' to empty away down the sluices – what a performance! Fortunately, there was a temporary shower block put up to the north of the classrooms for use after games.

1 Chatsworth, Derbyshire. The library piled high with
stored furniture in wartime.

2 Chatsworth, Derbyshire. The State Drawing Room as a dormitory in the occupation of Penrhos College, 1939. Painting by Edward Halliday

3 Chatsworth, Derbyshire. The Orangery in wartime

4 Castle Howard, Yorkshire. The dome burning, while
in the occupation of Queen Margaret's School from
Scarborough, 1940

5 Blenheim Palace, Oxfordshire. Boys from Malvern College in the Great Court, 1939

6 Blenheim Palace, Oxfordshire. The state rooms in use as a dormitory, 1939. The famous Flemish tapestries of the Duke of Marlborough's battles were left *in situ*

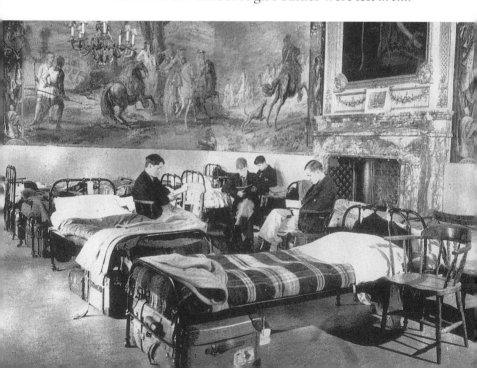

HERDOWN, DOWNTON HALL, LUDLOW.

7 Downton Hall, Shropshire. Postcard used by the boys of Heatherdown Prep School to send to their parents

8 Downton Hall, Shropshire. Photograph of the view from the house taken by the headmaster while in the occupation of Heatherdown School

9 Hatfield House, Hertfordshire. The King James
Drawing Room in use as a hospital ward

10 Hatfield House, Hertfordshire. The south front with
sandbags and the Dowager Marchioness of Salisbury

11 Carlton Towers, Yorkshire. Lady Beaumont with
voluntary helpers running the house as an auxiliary
military hospital

12 Mentmore, Buckinghamshire. Works of art from the
National Portrait Gallery stored in the Billiard Room,
1943

13 Woburn Abbey, Bedfordshire. The Riding School after
derequisitioning in 1947 with blackout curtains still
hanging in the windows

Several of the younger teaching staff were billeted in the laundry, and part of the Coach House was used to dry stinging nettle leaves (picked and individually placed on sacking shelves) for use in some drug-making process. The girls had to pick loads of rose hips in autumn and they were collected from the stables to be made into a syrup rich in vitamin C for babies.

The Orangery was used for art classes. In front of it in the formal knot garden, carrots, lettuces, etc. were grown inside the box hedges, not very successfully. Tennis courts were near the stables, but the main games pitches were across the lake and a long walk southwards.

Every Sunday the girls walked to Horningsham parish church, before breakfast for the early service, or after for the eleven am service.

Lord Bath, who lived alone, had an ancient dog and a young valet. He used to potter about the gardens and sometimes attended the school concerts, etc. I remember him standing with the girls ranged on either side of the front steps on the occasion of Queen Mary's visit, on 18 September 1943, for which the girls were rehearsed in the correct way to curtsey. We were given a 'free' half-holiday to mark the occasion.

The Royal School remained at Longleat from 1940 to 1945, but some of the girls returned the following year to pay their last respects after Lord Bath died on 9 June 1946. For the funeral they lined the steps, wearing their dark outdoor cloaks, making an appropriate, if unusual, guard of honour for the coffin when it left the house for the funeral procession to Horningsham church on the edge of the park.

Many Catholic owners of country houses invited convents to occupy their houses during the war. The Actons at Aldenham in Shropshire, for instance, arranged for the Convent of the Assumption and its school from Kensington Square, London, to share their house. Monsignor Ronald Knox also lived in the house during the war. He had retired as Catholic chaplain at Oxford in August 1939 and had arranged with Lord and Lady Acton to live in a cottage on their estate in order to concentrate on his great project of preparing a new Catholic translation of the Bible to replace the outdated Douay version. (This idea had been conceived originally by Newman in 1855, but had not hitherto been implemented.) The outbreak of war and the arrival of the convent put paid to any idea of peaceful retirement. Instead, he moved into the main house and acted as chaplain to the nuns and the children, but continued, nevertheless, with his great biblical project, most of which was written during the dark days of the war at Aldenham. Lord Acton was away, serving with his regiment. Lady Acton retained only the nursery and a dressing room for herself, together with a small sitting room at the front of the house which she shared with Knox. There they ate their meals and he kept his reference library and did his writing. The rest of the house was put at the disposal of the convent.

The first detachment from Kensington Square arrived on Friday, 1 September 1939, in the form of a charabanc containing ten nuns and six or seven foreign girls who had not gone home for the holidays. The rest of the school, about thirty girls, arrived three weeks later, after the furniture and other school equipment had been dispatched from London. At first, the nuns occupied the house according to a rather casual agreement. 'We were allowed the use of everything,' wrote the headmistress in 'News from Aldenham' in *The Assumption Chronicle War Issue No. 1* in April 1942. 'The home atmosphere remained in such lovely surroundings. The children were soon perfectly happy.' Lady Acton, however, who was heavily pregnant (her daughter Catherine – now Mrs Corbett – was born on 30 September 1939), was beset by anxieties about the gardeners' wages, leaks in the roof, and who was meant to be paying for what; and a more formal arrangement soon had to be agreed with the tenants. The Assumption nuns and their school stayed at Aldenham till Easter 1946 in a kind of *ménage à trois* with Lady Acton, who devoted her days to pig farming, and Monsignor Knox, who spent his time translating the Bible and saying mass for the convent 'in that unmistakable Oxford accent'.

While girls' schools in general did less damage than other forms of wartime use, not all the houses so occupied survived unscathed, as the terrible fate of Castle Howard demonstrated. It was occupied by Queen Margaret's School, a Woodard foundation from Scarborough, which was evacuated from the coast just in case the German Navy repeated its First World War bombardment of the harbour there. In November 1940, only a year after the school moved into Vanbrugh's masterpiece, the building was swept by a fire which is thought to have been caused by a fault in an electrically heated hot cupboard in the dining room on the south front, though rumour has always had it that the fire was begun by a homesick girl who wished to put an end to the school. The alert was given by a boy working on a farm on the estate who saw a red glow in the sky when he went out to see to the cows at five o'clock in the morning. The local fire brigade did not arrive till two hours later, by which time the south front was half gutted and the flames had engulfed the main dome which glowed like a beacon and sent cascades of molten lead splashing on to the marble floor of the Great Hall before itself crashing down. The roof over the six south front state rooms, used as classrooms, caved in, the whole centre of the house was gutted and most of Pellegrini's beautiful frescos destroyed. Mercifully, only a few of the contents were damaged. The best furniture had been removed to storage when the house was leased to the school, and much of the furniture was stacked in the Long Gallery in the Robinson Wing which the fire never reached.

Anne Hollis, who was a pupil at the time, wrote a vivid account of the fire:

It was Saturday, November 9th, 1940 at five-fifteen in the morning when I was awoken by somebody shaking my shoulder, and I heard the matron telling me, in a high-pitched, unnatural voice, to get up quickly and wake the rest of the bedroom. I sat up and listened, but I could hear not a sound; suddenly, however, I happened to glance out of the window, and I saw that the sky was a lurid crimson, and that the woods were lit up by the same brilliant light, and then I saw that the flames were pouring from the other side of the house. We all got dressed as we did for air raids – sweaters, socks, shoes and cloaks over our pyjamas, and our gas masks ready. I had heard no siren and no plane,

certainly no bomb, and I couldn't think what could
have caused such a blaze. We waited at the door
until the matron came back and told us to go down
to the air raid shelter. This we reached with the
help of wet sponges clasped to our faces, because
on leaving the bedroom we were surrounded by
dense and suffocating smoke. The air raid shelter
is a long broad space in the 'Underworld' with a
stone floor, stone walls, and a vaulted stone roof,
and somehow or other it seemed to be quite free
from smoke.

The sixth form helped to salvage some of the pictures:

We made our way up the stone steps into the
corridor which runs straight down the central
block and past the formrooms, and here we saw
the fire. The far end of the passage was ablaze
from floor to ceiling, and dull red smoke poured
down the corridor. Two figures were silhouetted
black against the ruddy light, and they looked
ridiculously small and helpless as they ran hither
and thither with buckets and stirrup pumps. We
went through two formrooms, until we reached
VA, the Reynolds Room, and here we found three
staff tugging at the pictures. The pictures in this
room were immense portraits, one of which took
up nearly a whole wall. There was no time to
unscrew the rails on which they were hung, and the
ladders that we had were not nearly long enough to
enable us to reach their tops, so we just had to tug at
them until the wires broke and they crashed on top
of us. We then took them into the Long Gallery,
which was at that time a safe distance from the

fire. Many of the pictures crashed from their frames when they fell, and the bare canvases were taken along to the Gallery. Somebody suggested getting into the studio and trying to rescue the priceless mirrors which hung there. On opening the door, however, we discovered that the fire had already claimed them, for it had reached the studio, and the windows and mirrors were cracked and falling in, while flames licked up the walls. By this time we had rescued all the pictures we could reach, and as the fire was steadily creeping on, we were sent down to the air raid shelter again. Fifteen minutes or so later, however, we had to be sent for again, for it looked as though nothing could prevent the fire from consuming everything, and the priceless old books in the Tapestry Room and corridor had to be saved at all costs. It was extraordinary how the flames had advanced even in this short time, for the fire was well up to the studio, and the whole of the lower end of the corridor was a blazing inferno. Red hot timbers were crashing from the roof, and through the haze of smoke and flame, we could see that the studio, VB formroom, the office, the headmistress's room and the dining room which contained several mirrors each worth £2,000, and several family portraits, were nothing but a smouldering ruin.

The girls were sent home for a short holiday after the fire, but then returned. The school continued to occupy the undamaged part of the house, and the sleeping quarters in the east wing were unaffected by the flames. The centre block and south-east state rooms, however, remained a gutted shell till after the war when the late George Howard returned to live in his family home and began the slow process of restoration which is still not completed.

Fewer boys' public schools were evacuated to country houses than girls' schools, but a small number were turned into migrants as a result of the requisitioning of their own buildings. Most of the public schools which were evacuated doubled up with other schools, rather than occupying country houses. Thus: Westminster School moved from London to Lancing on the Sussex Downs, Cheltenham to Shrewsbury and the City of London School to Marlborough. Rossall, however, moved from the Lancashire coast between Blackpool and Fleetwood to Naworth Castle, the seat of the Earl of Carlisle in Cumberland. The Oratory School moved from Reading, where its buildings were taken over by the government's radio monitoring unit, to Woodcote, a Georgian house near Henley where it has since remained. Malvern College in Worcestershire, which also had its buildings requisitioned by the government, migrated to Blenheim Palace at the invitation of the Duke of Marlborough. Four hundred boys spent a year there, before transferring to Harrow where they shared the school buildings for the remainder of the war. At Blenheim, the Marlborough family remained in the east wing, the Great Hall became the school dining room, the Long Library and state rooms became rather overcrowded dormitories, and the bedroom floor was converted to classrooms supplemented by temporary wooden huts in the grounds, while the old laundry served as the laboratory. Malvern at Blenheim was the only country-house contribution in the Second World War to which *Country Life* devoted an article along the lines of those which it had published in 1914.

By 1939, there was nothing extraordinary about a public school occupying a country house. Several major mansions had become new public schools on a permanent basis between the wars including Stowe, Canford and Bryanston, so there was a good precedent for the arrangement. The problem at Blenheim, as of the other occupied country houses, was not in adapting the place to school use *per se*, but in carrying out the conversion in the short space of time allowed, as Christopher Hussey explained in *Country Life* on 3 February 1940:

> The accommodation of four hundred boys and a hundred staff of various degrees and duties taxed even Blenheim's capacity and certainly had not been visualised by Blenheim's architect. Yet Vanbrugh's ghost must have chuckled with delight in having his belief at last confirmed that Blenheim is not an inch too big.

The story of the first four weeks is of the staff, hurriedly recalled, feverishly working at both ends over the tremendous business of removal. On 14 September, the first vans arrived at Blenheim and proceeded to dump their cargoes on the terrace. But the problem was complicated by the necessity of protecting those treasures in the state rooms that could not be moved for storage. As it was not found possible at such short notice to take down the pictures and the magnificent tapestries, the Duke decided that they should remain on the walls, and measures had to be taken against the risk of damage. Battens and screens of Essex board had to be fixed round the walls, the damask curtains protected with canvas covers, the great mahogany doors padded with felt, and the floors covered with 1,400 square yards of linoleum and 1,000 square yards of matting. All this preliminary work had to be done first, before the school's possessions could be installed. Meanwhile, great loads piled up on the terrace – fortunately, the weather was fine - while perishable objects, such as books and bedding, were heaped in the Great Hall. Then, when the rooms were ready to receive the furniture, the sorting-out process began: desks, beds, books, crockery, pianos, tables and great piles of unclassified and miscellaneous objects had to be taken to their destination. Hussey continues:

Apart from the move itself, there was a host of problems to be tackled. The kitchens could not cater for the numbers of the school; moreover, petrol gas was used for the ranges and would be unobtainable, so that a new gas main from Woodstock had to be laid. A gang of masters heroically set to work with picks and spades to dig a trench, half a mile long, in the Blenheim limestone, and were not sorry when a pneumatic drill arrived to take over. Besides extra cooking apparatus, new boilers had to be installed, and the ablutions of four hundred boys also had to be provided for. This problem was solved by fitting up a shower room in one of the internal courtyards. In another courtyard a changing-room was built of timber and Essex board, and fitted with seats, shelves and clothes racks for the games clothes of the whole school. The blackout also made its claims, no small ones in a building the size of Blenheim. Fortunately, all the state rooms were fitted with eighteenth-century shutters, but the Great Hall and the Long Library both had to be dealt with, besides a multitude of lesser lights. It took a small army of matrons and needlewomen to make Blenheim properly opaque by the opening of the term. Add to all this the detailed arrangements for the new life of the school, the adaptation of rooms to their new purposes, and innumerable minor problems – even the planting of goal-posts on the football pitches meant hours of work with crowbars and pick-axes, so solid is the rock on which Blenheim is built: consider all this and much more, and some idea can be gained of the magnitude of the achievement which made it possible for the school to re-assemble on October 9th, within five weeks of the start of operations.

More prep schools moved to country houses during the Second World War than did boys' public schools. And several of them have remained *in situ* ever since, such as, for example, the Abel-Smith's house at Woodhall Park, Hertfordshire. After the war the family did not move back in, but continued to let the big house to the school and in 1957 converted the stables into a more compact and comfortable residence for themselves.

A group of very important country houses became prep schools for the duration of the war, including Chicheley in Buckinghamshire and the Vyne in Hampshire. A less well-known example is Downton Hall in Shropshire (not to be confused with Downton Castle). This red-brick, early Georgian home of the Rouse-Boughton family played host to Camperdown

Prep School from Surrey. The owner, Sir Edward, had gone off to the war, but Lady Rouse-Boughton remained at Downton. There was no staff except for one aged retainer called Bishop who pumped the water and made the gas for the lighting, there being no electricity. The boys had the run of the whole of the wild and wooded estate, and the place seemed hardly like school at all. Lady Rouse-Boughton maintained the atmosphere of a private country house, though she herself remained aloof from the school and was rarely seen by the boys. David Clegg, who was at school at Downton, has written a short memoir of the place which captures the feel of the house, and many like it, during the war years:

Were it not for the Battle of Britain and the possibility of invasion, the opportunity to spend four years of the war in a remote corner of England would never have come about. The school moved from the horrid pine woods of outer suburbia to the heart of Shropshire. Its destination a little known landed estate.

In the unlikely event of stumbling across a Gothick gate lodge lost among lanes, a glimpse of a drive would be seen disappearing through thick woodlands. No park here, no sight of a house, only hidden promise. The drive, surprisingly, was found to wind through the woods for something approaching two miles, gradually climbing and changing direction along the side of a hill where golden and silver pheasants lived. Then round the final bend the great house revealed itself across open and undulating ground. Substantial and impressive, of red brick with stone dressings and standing on its terraced platform carved from the hillside. This then was the place which was to work powerfully on my imagination.

In spite of its sudden violation, the spirit of the place stayed unchanged. It retained its aura of quiet and settled peace and never became institutionalised. It remained a country house playing host to a very large house party for an unusually extended visit.

From the strictly architectural point of view, the house would not be considered distinguished. But its setting and surroundings were incomparable. The landscape gardener had laid only a light hand on it and relied on nature for the final effect. Looking south there unfolded a scene of extraordinary beauty unmarred by man. The natural lie of the land had much to do with this, gently falling away and framed by trees, then levelling into open country before finally ascending to the hills in the far distance. To the right and left under the terraces lay two lakes sheltered by trees, and to complete the picture woodlands behind the house climbed the hill giving shelter from the north.

Naturally, the most alluring places were out of bounds to boys. The private side, approached by the main staircase, was shared by the lady of the house and the headmaster and his wife. The only reason for a visit there was corporal punishment. Most of the furniture and pictures, on our arrival, had been taken to the saloon and remained there for the duration. This Aladdin's cave was never entered or unlocked and contained, one learnt many years later, some fine rococo plaster decoration. Then there was the muniment room near the back door, its purpose only suggested by the dimly discerned papers and vellum rolls showing through a dust-stained window high up on the wall. The back stairs gave on to the servants' quarters at the top of the house. Here were rooms given over to the lower forms and there were passages along one of which was a tiny and inaccessible door near the ceiling which gave access to attics and roof spaces. This and many other places denied to us were the province of the odd job man [Bishop] who nurtured an implacable hatred towards us. He was in charge of the oil engine in the yard which pumped the water for the house. Here also was the huge wooden game larder with louvred lantern, and further on the stable range. Unforgettable was the stable clock sounding the hours, particularly poignant in the dark of the night. The gas house at the edge of the woods was the cause of much speculation. The soft hissing of the gas lights shaded by obscured glass was one of the chief delights of the house after dark. Not surprisingly, the heating arrangements were largely wanting and we made do with ancient paraffin stoves whose main purpose was roasting chestnuts.

Other places remained entirely unknown and mysterious. A series of work shops heavily chained and padlocked contained untold treasures, tools of all sorts, benches, anvils, glue pots and much else. There were shadowy forms whose images could just be made out through foggy windows, long uncleaned. The walled kitchen garden at a lower level and to the west of the house was a closely guarded preserve containing peach and nectarine house and all kinds of soft fruit. Not even the most adventurous could penetrate this place.

Now, forty years on, the old house, happily, still lies unscathed and unchanged, the home of the family who have lived in this part of England for many generations.

Chapter IV
Hospitals

The contribution of country houses used as hospitals was not as significant in the Second World War as in the First. Military (and civilian) casualties were nothing like as great as feared, and not all the houses originally earmarked for hospital use were taken up. The tactics of war were swifter and more flexible thanks to the development of the tank, and there were, as a result, far fewer British wounded than in the trenches of the First World War. Nevertheless, a number of major country houses were transformed into military hospitals when war began. Several civilian hospitals were evacuated from London and the provincial cities in 1939, or later in the war, because of the fear of aerial bombardment. Many of the houses used as military hospitals were voluntarily offered by their owners, as they had been in the First World War, and the gesture was a belated instance of Victorian aristocratic public spiritedness. The Earl of Harewood and the Princess Royal offered Harewood House as a hospital for the use of wounded officers, Lady Beaumont and her husband, Lord Howard of Glossop, gave Carlton Towers as an overflow convalescent hospital for the York Military Hospital. Lady Baillie lent Leeds Castle in Kent, and Lord Joicey, Ford Castle in Northumberland. The 4th Marquess of Salisbury repeated his generosity of the First World War in the Second. He offered Hatfield House for use as a military hospital before the war started. An inscription in the chapel records: 'This house lent to the nation by the Marquis of Salisbury was established as a military hospital by the 13th (4th London) General Hospital RAMC TA 2nd September 1939'. In 1940 it was known as No. 24 (London) General Hospital, though the number changed again afterwards. It was always a military hospital and some Germans and other prisoners of war were treated there. There is a small War Graves Commission cemetery in Hatfield Park for those who died.

The furniture from the principal rooms at Hatfield was removed to storage, but the family portraits, armour and tapestries were left hanging on the walls. Protection works were kept to a minimum, most of the oak panelling and carved chimneypieces being left largely visible. The floors were covered with linoleum, and a few specially vulnerable features such as the painted eighteenth-century panels in the doors of the King James Drawing Room were protected with sheets of hardboard. A series of record photographs taken in December 1939 captures the look of the house then with rows of hospital beds in the ornate state rooms and Long Gallery, and white-uniformed orderlies mopping round the feet of impassive suits of armour in the Armoury. Look-out posts, constructed of sand bags, were erected outside the entrances and principal gateways, which gave the large Jacobean house a suitably workmanlike air.

Some of the houses lent as hospitals were initiated with some pomp. When Heath House in Staffordshire, for example, was turned into a hospital in 1939, there was a special opening ceremony at which the Bishop of Lichfield blessed the building, the staff, and the first batch of patients. Many country house hospitals retained something of the atmosphere of a stately home, the owner's wife often running the place herself, with the help of daughters and friends, which the patients appreciated. Margaret, Countess of Lichfield, recalls:

During the Second World War, Heath House – which belonged to my first husband, Humphrey Philips – and so many other country houses were turned into hospitals. The patients had the free run of Heath House, and loved and respected it and did all they possibly could to help. It seemed to bring the best out in all of them. They were always telling me that in the Army, Navy or Air Force, whichever they happened to be in, they all blasphemed in every sentence, everything 'bloody this' and 'bloody that', but there they found themselves never using any bad language in any shape or form – did not want to. They used to ask me why this was, they were so surprised. I pointed out to them that I had a collection of very young and pretty Red Cross nurses and they had too much respect for them to let themselves down in such a way, whether they knew it or not.

The result was delightful and for six years we did have a very happy hospital. Their letters and poems used to pour in after they had left. So these country houses and their lovely gardens played a very large part in the healing of men in mind, body and soul, when they came out of hell and found themselves in heaven.

At Carlton Towers in Yorkshire, Lady Beaumont, assisted by her daughter, Mariegold Fitzalan Howard, personally supervised the auxiliary hospital established there. On the outbreak of war the house was immediately offered to the York Military Hospital as an overflow convalescent hospital. Though military, it did not cater for wounded men and had no operating theatre in use; its purpose was to provide space for troops suffering from routine illnesses and epidemics: dysentery, pneumonia, shingles, appendicitis, sprains, concussion and so forth. It was staffed by five nurses, and a number of volunteer auxiliaries. Lady Beaumont ran it, and her daughters and friends helped with the cooking and similar tasks. There was a permanent fire-fighting picket of five men based in the stables. This was rather a waste of manpower but one insisted on by the authorities, and a feature of many of the country houses taken over during the war.

Preparations for the hospital were elaborate. The paintings were left hanging on the walls, but all the furniture from the house was removed, packed up, and stored throughout the war in a warehouse in York. There a number of items including a large billiards table went missing, and some of the fine Victorian fabrics designed by J.F. Bentley (the architect of Westminster Cathedral, who was responsible for the interior fitting out of Carlton Towers in the 1870s), including the hangings on all the four-poster beds, were eaten by moths; moths in general spent a very well-fed war. The carved woodwork and painted decorations in the state rooms were protected to a height of about eight feet by hardboard panelling. All this took some time to complete, but the place was fully operational on 1 September 1939, and remained in use till 1 October 1945.

The Victorian state rooms were adapted as interconnecting wards, the state bedrooms lining the long passage behind were transformed into bathrooms and other subsidiary accommodation. The upper floors were occupied as billets for the doctors, nurses and auxiliaries. The dining room was used as a mess by the auxiliary staff. The family retreated to two rooms in the old wing, where they used the Morning Room as their sitting room and the adjoining Harp Room as their private dining room. Lady Beaumont kept a register in which she recorded the names and other details of the 3,000 patients who passed through, followed by her own short comments in red ink: 'Cheeky'; 'Noisy and a communist'; 'Nothing wrong at all'; 'Harmless'; 'Reads Sir Walter Scott'; 'Nice red-headed giant. Only eats potatoes'; 'Missed Mass twice'; 'Drunk'; 'Can't read or write. Nice lout'; 'Very tiresome – Complaining of food'; 'Quite potty'; 'Nice quiet boy'; 'No teeth. Nice. Oldish. Looks a villain'. She also recorded the patients' jokes: 'Says he's returned to his country residence for Easter'; 'Home from home'.

Other country houses used as military convalescent homes included Hawkstone Park in Shropshire, Preston Hall (Kent), Lynford Park (Norfolk), Stapleford Park (Leicestershire), Picton Castle (Wales), Sandhill Park (Somerset), and Crossrigg Hall (Cumberland). The owner of the latter, Commander Richard Torbock, remembers the wartime occupation of the house which is Victorian, designed in the Jacobean style by Anthony Salvin. At the beginning of the war it was filled with refugees from Gateshead.

But following the death of his mother, this use had to be given up because the old lady had personally looked after the children, all the staff having been called up and both Commander Torbock and his younger brother, Cornish, were themselves away at war. So the house was then offered as a convalescent home for Dominion officers. Most of the contents were left in place, and it was lived in as if it were still a private house. This proved very successful and hardly any damage was caused apart from one cracked washbasin in the downstairs cloak room, in which something was dropped by accident. Commander Torbock says that he would be happy to offer the house again for the same use if there were another war.

During the First World War Harewood House had been a convalescent hospital for officers wounded in action, and on the outbreak of the Second World War in 1939, Lord Harewood immediately made the greater portion of the house available for the same purpose. He and his wife, the Princess Royal, retreated to the east wing which had its own staircase and could therefore be sealed off from the rest of the house to form a self-contained unit. The exceptionally fine collection of paintings, including two Titians, an El Greco and several important early Italian panels, as well as the more usual country house contents, and unique documented Chippendale furniture made to Adam's design were all packed up and carefully stored. The superb Adam state rooms were protected in the usual way with linoleum and hardboard. To make a convenient entrance for the hospital staff and patients, the venetian window at the north end of the Gallery was removed and a makeshift door made there, protected from the weather by a temporary canopy. The hospital used the main kitchen in the basement of the house, cooking on a vast Victorian cast-iron range. A smaller independent kitchen was made for the family in the housekeeper's room in the west wing where an Esse cooker was used, 'but the journey across the basement and up to the Breakfast Room [used as the private dining room] on the east side offset the convenience of the more modern stove'. Harewood remained in operation as a hospital till the end of the war. James Lees-Milne visited on 26 November 1947 as it was being put to rights again, and jotted down his impressions of the rooms being cleaned, the venetian window being reinstated at the end of the Gallery, and the Adam rooms being put back to their pre-war condition, with Chippendale furniture, Old Master paintings and Sèvres porcelain, very little damage having been inflicted by the officers who had occupied the place.

Many other houses were military hospitals of one sort or another. Bradfield Park in Berkshire, the seat of the Walrond family; Vaynol in North Wales, the home of Sir Michael Duff; Cornwell Manor in Oxfordshire; The Park at Wimpole in Cambridgeshire; Capesthorne in Cheshire; Ashridge in Hertfordshire; Somerleyton in Suffolk; and Corsham Court in Wiltshire were all occupied by hospitals, some naval, some Red Cross, some American. At Corsham, the Methuens retreated to the Gothic library where they lived and ate their meals while all the state rooms were occupied by wards. Only a portion of the splendid contents were put away. The highly important paintings were left on the walls, and the gilt pier tables and other fragile eighteenth-century furniture was left in the rooms. James Lees-Milne on a visit on 23 May 1945 was distressed to see 'the hospital orderlies banging the furniture with the backs of their brooms'.

As well as military hospitals, several ordinary, civilian hospitals were also evacuated to country houses. At the beginning of the war, many hospitals with long-term patients and maternity homes were moved from the more congested central areas of the cities for the same reasons as school children, orphans and poor families were evacuated, to protect them from the imminent prospect of aerial bombardment. These moves were partly organised by the Ministry of Health, and partly by the County Councils. Several houses in the counties near London were occupied by hospitals evacuated from the East End. Brocket in Hertfordshire, for instance, became a maternity hospital, and Lord Brocket himself moved into Warren House on the other side of the lake in the park. Battlesden Abbey in Bedfordshire was taken over by Bedfordshire County Council in 1939 as a maternity hospital. Stockwood Park in Bedfordshire was occupied by the Alexandra Hospital from Luton. The same pattern was repeated in other areas of the country. In the West Riding of Yorkshire, for example, several eighteenth-century mansions, including Stockeld Park (designed by James Paine) and Farnley Hall (designed by John Carr of York) became maternity homes evacuated from the big industrial towns nearby.

A further wave of emigration of hospitals to the country took place towards the end of the war in the face of German rocket attacks on London. Dr

W.E. Snell, who was the medical superintendent at Colindale Hospital, Hendon, remembers how his hospital was evacuated at that time to Kinmel Hall near Abergele in North Wales, the large, late nineteenth-century 'Queen Anne Revival' mansion of the Hughes family. He recollects that in 1944 fear of an imminent rocket attack influenced the London County Council, which was then in charge of all London hospitals except teaching hospitals, to move all long-stay patients from London. The Colindale Hospital, which contained 250 to 300 beds for patients suffering from TB (consumption) was given the choice of various buildings in different parts of the country.

Dr Snell chose Kinmel because his wife and family had been evacuated to Northampton and he could easily visit them there by train from Abergele via Crewe. Kinmel had already been adapted as a hospital by the army and so was immediately available without any further alterations. They fitted in about two hundred TB patients in the large ground floor reception rooms there and on the principal bedroom floor. The hospital staff were given segregated accommodation on the upper floors, while some twenty porters were accommodated in the stable block. Their evacuation to Kinmel proved to be a necessary precaution as five or six bombs fell on Colindale completely destroying one wing of the hospital. At Kinmel, they were able to provide all the treatments then known for TB, and the sea air on the north Welsh coast was in any case beneficial to the patients.

Once he was established at Kinmel, Dr Snell was soon able to take a house for his wife and two children at Rhyl, the nearby seaside resort, and stayed there with them, cycling back and forth to the hospital. Mrs Snell remembers the return journey to London at the end of the war. The toy chest and heavy luggage was sent to London ahead of the rest of the party. Dr Snell drove back with the remainder of the luggage in his own car and his wife and children went back by train:

We left in a Rolls Royce taxi and joined a special evacuees' train which took evacuee children, and hospital staff – doctors, nurses, porters, etc. – that were not needed on the ambulance train carrying the patients. My husband saw the ambulance train off after we had gone, and then left by car at twelve noon, arriving at seven-fifteen pm at Colindale Hospital, Hendon. We had a normal train journey back, except that we had ordered a taxi to meet us at one London station (I forget which), but owing to wartime hush-hush still being in operation for some reason, we couldn't find out where we were going, and eventually ended up at five-thirty pm at Euston, where fortunately a coach was waiting for the staff and there was room for us, so we went back with them to Colindale.

Chapter V
Museums

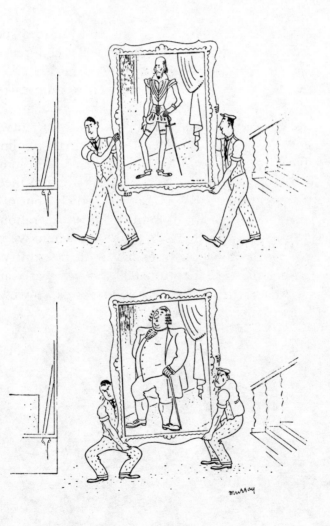

As early as 1935 a meeting was called by the Office of Works to consider what to do with the contents of the national museums in wartime. As Sir Henry Hake, director of the National Portrait Gallery, put it: 'This meeting gave an opportunity for the assembled officials to rehearse their relationships and acquaintances in country houses.' Nor was it just snobbery which made large mansions seem the obvious places for museum curators to consider storing the nation's art treasures during an emergency. The boards of trustees of many museums had a fair sprinkling of the owners of such properties among their members, and many Georgian seats were at least partly designed for the display of art collections. To eke out the supply of country houses, the government also earmarked a number of railway tunnels for museum storage, including Dover Street and Aldwych Underground stations and the Newlands railway tunnel in the Forest of Dean, Monmouthshire.

At the meeting in 1935, the Office of Works suggested an overall plan of evacuation for the contents of the principal London museums and art galleries, perhaps using Hampton Court Palace as an evacuation staging area by all the institutions involved. This idea was not favourably received by the curators, and instead it was accepted that each individual museum should make its own approaches among 'its clientele of country residences'. The major London museums began to make their own detailed arrangements for evacuating their collections before the Munich crisis in 1938.

Many private owners were delighted at the prospect of storing famous pictures and other works of art in their houses rather than playing reluctant host to noisy, messy, evacuee children. James Lees-Milne, in his wartime diaries, tells the story of Henley Hall in Shropshire where the contents of Blickling Hall, Norfolk, were stored for safe-keeping. The owner's wife confided to him in July 1942: 'If there is any threat of evacuees, I shall spread out the art treasures . . . into more rooms.'

The 'treasures' when they turned up, packed in bulky wooden crates, often turned out to be less alluring than was anticipated. Evelyn Waugh in *Men at Arms* describes the reaction of Guy Crouchback's sister Angela Box-Bender to the museum objects stored in her fictional Cotswold house:

Drawing room and dining room were blocked to the ceiling with wooden crates. 'Such a disappointment, darling,' said Angela. 'I thought we'd been so clever. I imagined us having the Wallace Collection and luxuriating in Sèvres and Boulle and Bouchers. Such a cultivated war, I imagined. Instead we've got the Hittite tables from the British Museum, and we mayn't even peep at them, not that we want to, heaven knows . . . All the Prentice's evacuees have gone back to Birmingham in a huff,' said Angela. 'They always were unnaturally lucky. We've got the Hittite horrors for life, I know.'

In reality the Wallace Collection was evacuated to West Wycombe Park, the eighteenth-century seat of the Dashwoods in Buckinghamshire. The National Trust office and records were also moved to West Wycombe from their London premises in Buckingham Palace Gardens at the beginning of the war, till it was deemed safe enough for them to return in 1943. The staff both of the Wallace Collection and of the National Trust, together with a transient population of paying guests, including Eddie Sackville-West and Nancy Mitford, also lodged in the house. The National Trust offices occupied the Brown Drawing Room and Sir John Dashwood's study. The Wallace Collection filled the Blue Drawing Room and the Music Saloon, while its curators lived in part of the damp and derelict old servants' wing at the back of the house. The Yellow Drawing Room was used as a communal refectory for all the occupants of the house till 1942, when it too was taken over for the storage of works of art, namely Sir Robert Witt's collection from London (now part of the Courtauld Institute Gallery). From then on meals were eaten in the servants' hall in the basement, and only one room on the ground floor, the Tapestry Room, was left as a sitting room for the assorted denizens of the place.

It must have been the most extraordinary ménage, with Eddie Sackville-West playing the piano in the hall and enjoying ill health surrounded at his place in the dining room by a collection of eighteenth-century snuff boxes full of different kinds of pills;

James Lees-Milne of the National Trust and Nancy Mitford reading aloud from biographies while knitting socks, and teasing their hostess Lady Dashwood about the cold of the house and the eccentric wartime food. Nancy Mitford christened the upstairs lavatory 'the Beardmore' after the Antarctic, James Lees-Milne recalls:

> Before luncheon, Nancy said, 'I must just go to the Beardmore . . .' 'The what?' Helen asked. 'Don't you know,' we said, 'that the upstairs lavatory is called after the Beardmore Glacier. It faces due north. The window is permanently propped open so that it can't be shut, and the floor is under a drift of snow.' Helen doesn't find this a funny joke.

The food was equally odd and unpredictable. Sir Francis Dashwood, who was a schoolboy at the time, recalls that in order to eke out small wartime rations:

> We resorted to eating coots and moorhens which were cooked in aspic and served cold. On one occasion we even decided to shoot a swan.

James Lees-Milne remembers the lugubrious butler serving Lady Dashwood on this occasion, announcing with a straight face, 'Swan or sucking pig, milady?'
Sometimes, to further enliven the evenings, the curators of the Wallace Collection would get out one or two choice Watteaus, Bouchers or Fragonards for everybody to gloat over, or a few pieces of Sèvres or ormolu or a lapis lazuli snuff box or

14 Penrhyn Castle, Wales. Van Dyck's large equestrian portrait of Charles I from the National Gallery arriving, September 1939

15 Wilton House, Wiltshire. Independence Day garden party, 4 July 1943. The pipe band of the Highland Light Infantry entertaining the guests

16 Wilton House, Wiltshire. Lt.-Gen. Auchinleck and allied officers with Lord and Lady Pembroke, 23 September 1940

17 Arundel, Sussex. Tanks on the Sussex Downs on the
Duke of Norfolk's estate, near Arundel Castle,
12 August 1940

18 Holkham Hall, Norfolk. The numbers and names of
tanks painted above their parking spaces on the wall of
the kitchen court

19 'The stalls of the stables are reminiscent of the old London coffee houses.' Military Police Company mess in a stable block, Wiltshire, 25 November 1940

20 Longford Castle, Wiltshire. 5th Corps, Southern Command practising camouflage in the grounds, 17 December 1940

21 Coleorton, Leicestershire. HRH The Princess Royal inspects the ATS in front of the house

22 Wentworth Woodhouse, Yorkshire. General Sir Bernard Paget on a tour of inspection of the Intelligence Corps Depot in Northern Command, 27 August 1943

23 Brucklay Castle, Banffshire. Pipe band playing the retreat during a tour of inspection by HRH The Duchess of Gloucester, Colonel-in-Chief of the King's Own Scottish Borderers

24 Glenfinnan House, Scotland. In occupation as HMS Armadillo 1945, one of the Combined Operations bases on the west coast of Scotland

25 Rosneath Castle, Dunbartonshire. In occupation as a
Combined Operations base, 1945

26 Tullichewan Castle, Scotland. Wrens' quarters, 1945

27 Eaton Hall, Cheshire. Royal Naval College,
Dartmouth, 1945. Cadets' houses in the forecourt

28 Eaton Hall, Cheshire. Royal Naval College divisions
with inspection taken by Capt. G. H. Warner,
Commanding Officer of the college, 1945

two. Seeing one of the latter reminded Nancy Mitford of a story of an American millionaire's wife who, meeting a parson's daughter wearing a small necklace of lapis lazuli remarked, 'I have a staircase made of those.'

The director of the National Portrait Gallery, Sir Henry Hake and H.I. Kay, at that time keeper of the National Gallery, made a joint exploration of country houses before the Munich crisis to try to find accommodation to share. Their first choice was Mentmore in Buckinghamshire, a seat of Lord Rosebery, because they had previously met and kept up an acquaintance with Lord Rosebery's agent, Charles Edmunds. In the event, the National Gallery decided that Mentmore did not offer the type of accommodation which they required, but the National Portrait Gallery did move there for the duration of the war. Sir Henry Hake, in 1943, wrote a short personal narrative of the transfer and storage of the collection of 1,457 pictures from St Martin's Place to Mentmore, which is worth quoting at length as it gives an on-the-spot view of this episode:

When the Munich crisis was on us I rang up Mr Edmunds and asked him if he could provide a refuge for a few of our more important pictures. This he said he could do. Nothing was moved at this time, but it was clear after Munich that serious thought would have to be given to plans for protection and evacuation. A priority list of sixty items for immediate evacuation was drawn up and approved by the trustees.

The Office of Works constructed a strong room in the basement large enough to hold six hundred pictures without their frames; this became known as the dug-out.

During the winter and spring of 1938–39 we made a number of experiments in packing, using old students' copies; we also tested packing materials – for example, a parcel of canvases wrapped in waterproof paper was left out in the snow for a fortnight.

Most important of all, we made the pictures in the collection more easily movable by fitting the panels with narrow guard frames and substituting spring catches for the nails holding the pictures in the frames. There was not time to treat all the larger pictures.

As a further help to mobility, the system of fixing the pictures on the walls was changed to a hook and eye fixing in place of a cord fixing through two eyes. This made it possible to disengage the pictures in less than half the usual time.

I asked Mr Edmunds at Mentmore if he could find us a place for our pictures in the event of war. He finally offered us a group of outbuildings known as the gas house which had begun by housing the gas-making apparatus for the estate and later for making the electric light. The battery room, as it was called, was a brick building 32 x 16 feet (inside) with a concrete floor and a tiled roof lined with thick match boarding.

This we took over, calling it the refuge and during the spring of 1939 the house carpenter stayed at Mentmore for a week and built timber racks which Mr Adams had calculated for the different sizes of pictures without their frames. We also installed four low temperature electric pipe heaters.

We next made plans for the actual move: orders were issued for men to stand by to accompany the pictures; and we finally arranged with the Office of Works to let us employ our usual transport contractor whom the attendants knew personally and who had proved to be a careful driver; I told my colleagues that all of us would take a month's holiday and be back on duty by the 1st September and this was done.

On the evening of 23rd August, I was rung up by the Office of Works to say that the First Commissioner had obtained a permissive instruction from the Home Office for museums to evacuate. The Gallery was closed on August 24th, and our move began the same day. I ordered a van for two o'clock and the sixty items of first importance were stacked ready for loading before one. The van left with an escort and two guards who were to stay at Mentmore. Mr Edmunds rang me up at my house soon after six to say that the pictures had arrived.

Evacuation went on steadily. In due time living quarters for the men at the refuge had to be made less primitive. They had begun with two home-made camp beds and a few cooking pots. The outbuilding had been wired for electricity and an electric cooking stove was put in within a week of their arrival. During the autumn of 1939, the house carpenter fitted up the outer room of the building with sleeping bunks; a coke stove was put in for heating and the unlined tiled floor was lined with composition packing.

I stayed for two nights in a nearby cottage early in November and made sure that both pictures and men were properly housed for the coming winter.

The rule had been laid down that all four men must sleep in the refuge at night and that never less than two must be on duty in the daytime. Gradually life at the refuge got organised and a system of fortnightly reliefs was instituted. One man who was a native of Buckinghamshire asked to stay permanently and became housekeeper and cook. A vegetable garden was got under way. Chickens appeared later on.

One senior attendant was placed in charge of the refuge and did a period of duty of six weeks at a time, with reliefs of a fortnight by the head attendant from London. In this way, the organisation grew under the joint guidance of the head attendant and attendant in charge at Mentmore. I made fairly frequent visits and with Mr Adams set about closing down our peacetime activities in London.

After Dunkirk, I asked Mr Edmunds whether he could provide me with some form of quarters in case I thought it necessary to be there myself. He found the visiting grooms' quarters of the hunting stables and these I occupied with my wife during the month of July 1940. The same quarters were occupied by Mr Adams and his family during August. The Battle of Britain had begun in August and the night raids started in September. On October 15th I decided to move my wife down to the hunting stables and moved myself into the National Portrait Gallery; for eighteen months from this date I divided my time between the two places.

The pictures had been packed for the first move in a very summary fashion to ensure lightness and mobility. The canvases had been taken out of their frames and packed according to their sizes, face to face with corks at the corners held in place by panel pins. The edges of the canvases and the backs of the outer ones were protected with sheets of three-ply which had been specially ordered and cut before-hand. This meant that one, two or three pairs of paintings could be made into a compact and self-contained bundle weighing very little more than the canvases themselves. Panels were similarly packed with tissue paper and carpet felt. It was not a form of packing which allowed of any unpacking and repacking, so we decided gradually to undo all the bundles and provided each picture with a tempo-rary frame made of planed American whitewood, 2 x 1 inches. This job was carried out at Mentmore by the NPG's own house carpenter during the course of the year 1942.

The portraits from the Speaker's House in the Pal-ace of Westminster were also stored at Mentmore throughout the war. And early in 1941 the Office of Works transported there some of the treasures from the Royal collections. The eighteenth-century state coach, designed by Sir William Chambers, was moved from the Royal Mews at Buckingham Palace to the coach house at Mentmore, and the tapes-tries, furniture and Grinling Gibbons carvings from Hampton Court Palace were stored in the large cen-tral hall of the main house, the laundry and in two loose-boxes at the stud farm at Grafton. These, too, were looked after by the National Portrait Gallery staff.

Life at Mentmore was not entirely uneventful. Six bombs were dropped in the park in the late summer of 1940, and two land-mines fell and exploded about a mile away on the night of 17/18 November 1940. In July 1940 the National Portrait Gallery staff (to the subsequent horror of the Office of Works) demolished the tall chimneystack of the gas house, at a cost of £42, in order to remove the risk of it collapsing as a result of an explosion on to some of the paintings stored below.

In the summer of 1942, 221 of the most important paintings were moved from Mentmore to underground storage in the British Museum's depot at the Westwood Bath Stone Quarry near Bradford-on-Avon, and some lesser paintings which had been left stacked in a ground floor corridor of the Gallery building in St Martin's Place were in turn transferred to Mentmore to fill their space. At the same time, the finest picture frames were also moved from London and stacked in the billiard room at Mentmore together with the sculpture from the Gallery, such as the electrolyte copies of the royal effigies on the tombs in Westminster Abbey.

The collections remained at Mentmore till 1945 when they were taken back to London and rehung in the Gallery immediately after VE Day. By that time the staff had become rather dug in, and were loathe to leave Buckinghamshire. The Mentmore estate was sad, too, to see them go. The agent, Charles Edmunds, wrote to Sir Henry Hake on 30 September 1945:

Six years is a long time; at the commencement of the stay we were all strangers to one another; the end of it was the parting of real friends; the whole parish will join in this. You will all be missed. I want you to thank your side not only for their friendship, but also for what friendship implies; the willingness to help one another in so many ways and fitted in so well with our village life. Any of you will always be welcome if ever they pay us a visit. The stay here of the NPG was one of the bright spots in a time of universal sorrow and trouble.

The National Gallery, having decided against Mentmore as being too near London and not big enough for its collection, focused its sights on a range of other country houses. Kenneth Clark, who was then the director, recalled in the second volume of his autobiography, *The Other Half*, the difficulties which the Gallery faced in finding somewhere suitable. 'England is full of large houses, and I thought it would be easy to find a proprietor who would have welcomed the quiet occupation of his house by famous pictures rather than by rowdy and incontinent evacuees.' But the right mixture of attributes proved frustratingly elusive. The ideal location had to be near a town and railway station, yet remote enough to be free from the threat of bombing. It also had to have a door or window large enough to admit Van Dyck's vast equestrian portrait of King Charles I.

In 1938, in consultation with the Air Ministry, the Gallery decided to concentrate its search on North Wales as the safest area for the paintings to be moved to. A number of houses, castles and halls were inspected and approved by the Office of Works; arrangements were also made with the local British Legion for the provision of guards to supplement the Gallery's own depleted staff. Penrhyn Castle was chosen as the major repository because it was the only place able to take the large Van Dyck. Its coach house had six doors of enormous height which would easily admit all the largest canvases in the collection. Some of the smaller pictures were scattered in different depositories in the area, including the Prichard-Jones Hall of Bangor University, the National Library of Wales at Aberystwyth, Caernarvon Castle, Plas-y-Bryn at Bontnewydd, and Crosswood, the Earl of Lisburne's house near Aberystwyth. The intention was to spread the risk as far as possible.

At Penrhyn Castle, as well as the coach house, the dining room was used to house the paintings, for which purpose it was well suited because the heavy wooden shutters in the windows kept out climatic variations and made it possible to maintain the stable environment vital to the well-being of the pictures. To this end, the Office of Works installed electric panel heaters in the room. It was in these conditions that the Gallery's restoration staff embarked on a grand programme of cleaning the paintings, then a rather controversial thing to do.

Back in 1938 it was agreed that the pictures should be transported by rail. Kenneth Clark, in his lofty way, acknowledged the contribution of Ian Rawlins, the head of the Gallery's scientific department and 'one of the most relentless bores I have ever encountered. He was a railway-train addict . . . he read Bradshaw every night.' When it came to planning the removal of the paintings, he knew exactly what lines were available and what hours were free for a special train. In the two years leading up to the outbreak of the war the pictures were adapted to make their removal speedier and easier.

The frames of all the larger pictures were adapted so that the pictures could be removed in a narrow slip, leaving the frame on the wall. An additional lift was put in to give further access from the exhibition rooms to the ground floor. A dock with a sliding shutter door was made at the end of a ground floor room for loading the containers, and a concrete road laid across the yard to this and another door, already existing, which also was to be used for loading, as the ground is uneven and often very soft. In this way it was possible to load two containers at the same time. Frequent practices were held for the staff and a small body of volunteers in removing the pictures from the walls, and a few rehearsals with the well-wagons in loading the big cases.

The Munich crisis provided the opportunity for a full dress rehearsal. All the paintings were taken down from the walls of the Gallery, packed up and sent off by train under the care of Neil MacLaren, one of the young keepers who had already had some experience of a project of this type, having helped to evacuate the art collection from the Prado in Madrid during the Spanish Civil War. The story goes that at Crewe the National Gallery train was met by the station master, dressed in top hat, frock coat, gold watch chain and flower in his button hole. He told the keeper and staff that war had been averted for the time being and they were to return to London.

Most of the paintings were transported door-to-door in standard railway containers, but specially designed 'elephant' cases were built by the Office of Works for a dozen of the larger items. All except one were 'within gauge' and could pass under all the bridges and tunnels. The exception was the Van Dyck of Charles I, and a triangular conveyance had to be constructed for this so that it could be transported at an angle, the only way of getting it through the various arches *en route*. All the pictures made the journey without mishap, and arrived safely at Bangor, thanks to the efficiency of Ian Rawlins and an 'admirable railway man called Inspector Bagshaw'. The first load left London on 23 August 1939, and the last on 2 September, so that the whole collection had been successfully evacuated before the declaration of war. Kenneth Clark was also Surveyor of the King's Pictures, and the most important paintings from Buckingham Palace and Hampton Court were evacuated alongside the National Gallery collection to Wales for the duration of the war.

Following the fall of France, North Wales, which hitherto had been beyond the range of enemy aircraft, found itself vulnerable to aerial bombardment. The proximity of Liverpool, where the docks were an obvious war target, meant that it was not beyond the bounds of possibility that a stray bomber might unload over Penrhyn Castle. Following the bombing of Coventry, various places in Bangor were also commandeered for essential war manufacturing purposes, and the Ministry of Aircraft Production proposed to take over part of the ground floor of Penrhyn Castle itself for offices. The National Gallery was worried about this, as it threatened to turn their safe refuge into a legitimate target for the enemy. Some of the trustees wished to send the pictures to Canada, but Kenneth Clark thought they should remain in Britain. He consulted the Prime Minister who replied in red ink: 'Bury them in the bowels of the earth, but not one picture shall leave this island. WSC.' Once again, Ian Rawlins proved indispensable. He discovered a huge underground slate quarry, the Manod near Blaenau Ffestiniog, and all 2,000 of the National Gallery's pictures were transferred there after suitable adaptation in August 1941, leaving Penrhyn Castle in the hands of the Ministry of Aircraft Production.

The British Museum made similar arrangements for evacuation to those of the National Portrait Gallery and the National Gallery. In the early stages of war a number of country houses were taken over for storage including Compton Wynyates in Warwickshire, the Tudor house of the Marquess of Northampton, and Boughton, Northamptonshire, the great francophile baroque house of the Duke of Buccleuch, while the drawings and prints were evacuated to the National Library of Wales in Aberystwyth. The use of country houses was, however, only a temporary measure pending the construction of large-scale purpose-built underground storage in the Bath stone quarries at Westwood near Bradford-on-Avon, to which the bulk of the collections were moved in 1941. The paintings from Kenwood and a large part of the contents of the Victoria and Albert Museum were also transferred there for safe-keeping. Prior to this, the latter had evacuated a selection of the finest objects in the museum to Montacute in Somerset, the property of the National Trust, on the declaration of war in 1939.

The Tate Gallery took over Muncaster Castle, situated on the remote Cumberland coast, the seat of the Pennington-Ramsdens, and Sudely Castle in Gloucestershire. The London Museum adopted the Piccadilly Underground shelter as its main store, but

evacuated forty cases of objects to Ascott in Buckinghamshire, a late nineteenth-century, timber-framed
house of the Rothschilds, where they were stored
in the large cricket pavilion alongside the treasures
from the London synagogues which Anthony de
Rothschild had also agreed to have for the duration of the war. (The main house at Ascott was
used as a convalescent home.) The Natural History
Museum also evacuated its collections to various
country houses, including the fifteenth-century tower
of Tattershall Castle in Lincolnshire, another property of the National Trust. James Lees-Milne, who
visited Tattershall in 1942, found the rooms filled
with stacks of fossils 'neatly packed. The whole
place reeks of mothballs.' Despite the care with
which they were packed and stored, it was later
claimed that the wartime migration of some of
the more fragile exhibits, like butterflies and stuffed
animals, had had 'disastrous effects on the specimens
so stored'.

At the Public Record Office in Chancery Lane,
Munich helped to concentrate minds on the plans
for evacuation of the contents in case of war. A plan
of action was drawn up. All the records were to be
packed according to category and moved out to the
country according to their age and importance, beginning with the contents of the museum which included
such national treasures as the Domesday Book (sent
to Somerset), the most modern documents being
moved out last to places nearer London. The bulk
of material was divided into three lots. The Duke
of Rutland, who was keenly interested in historical
archives, offered to store as many as he could in his
two large houses in the Midlands, medieval Haddon

Hall in Derbyshire and the Regency Gothic Belvoir Castle in Leicestershire. It was necessary, according to the rules of the Public Record Office, that the documents should have an official curator to look after them, so the Duke was made a Public Record Office curator for the war years. The other major batch of documents destined for a country house went to Clandon in Surrey, the large eighteenth-century house of the Earl of Onslow, under the direction of Noel Blakiston, one of the Public Record Office staff. This, too, was the result of personal acquaintance. Noel Blakiston knew the Onslows and asked them whether the Public Record Office could move to their house when war broke out. Lord Onslow agreed, and the Blakiston family moved there, with the documents, and lived in the house for six years. The archives were stored chiefly in the Great Hall and Saloon, two vast rooms, where they were piled to the ceiling in crates and covered with tarpaulins to keep out the dust. Only one sitting room was left on the ground floor, and meals were eaten in the basement. Merida Drysdale, who was a friend of the Blakiston children, remembers being invited to stay with them at Clandon and playing hide-and-seek in the narrow gangways between the mountain of crates, and also the intense cold of the house, for there was no heating and the bedrooms were reached down what seemed miles of freezing passages.

The *éminence grise* who masterminded the wartime removal of 2,000 tons of archives from the Public Record Office in London and their restoration afterwards without a single loss was Sir David Evans. The task involved sending 600 van loads containing 100,000 cartons and bundles to the locations outside

London, which had no shelf space to match the thirty miles of shelving in Chancery Lane. As well as the three country houses other smaller repositories included a Somerset prison! And at the end of the war Sir David went down to Shepton Mallet gaol himself for the Domesday Book which he brought back, wrapped up beside him in an unmarked van.

As well as the major museums and repositories, many of the smaller collections were also evacuated from London. Even the rather sleepy Sir John Soane's Museum in Lincoln's Inn Fields moved its contents to country houses by slow degrees. In August 1939, twenty-one of the more valuable paintings and four cases of the manuscripts and drawings were sent to the National Gallery and British Museum for transfer with their collections to the country for safe-keeping, but no arrangements were at first made for the remaining contents. On the night of 8 September 1940, most of the windows and skylights in the Museum were blown in by air blast as a land mine struck the south-east corner of Lincoln's Inn Fields, and later on 24 September a firebomb shot through the plyboarding of the back window in the library on the ground floor. Very little stirred at the Soane, however, until September in the following year when the trustees began to discuss the possibilities of evacuating the contents of the Museum. Lord Crawford offered to store a certain number of cases at his house near Wigan, Haigh Hall. Accordingly, on 2 December 1941, two vans containing all the architectural drawings, documents and selected books started off, stopping on the way at Northampton before blackout, where one man slept in the van. They arrived next day at Haigh Hall, where the cases were all stored in a brick-vaulted cellar. The Museum had to pay a rental of £54.6s.0d. per annum plus heating costs.

The trustees had wanted to keep the collection together, but that had proved impossible. Consequently, they accepted Sir Harry Verney's generous offer to take the remainder, if the Museum paid the heating bills, and there was also a small rental of £15.0s.0d. per annum. His house, Rhianva, was on Anglesey, and the cases were to be stored in his tenants' hall. Between 9 and 23 February 1942, ten vans, each making a three-day trip of 500 miles, went up to Anglesey; they took with them 250 tea chests and 22 specially constructed wooden cases which contained furniture, paintings, framed architectural drawings, models and the smaller marbles. The casts and larger marbles were left in the Museum. Both groups of material were returned by March 1946.

The College of Arms moved its library, unique collection of heraldic records and historical portraits as well as the carved woodwork from the Earl Marshal's Court to Thornbury Castle in Gloucestershire, the medieval country house of the then Garter King of Arms, Sir Algar Howard. When they returned to the College at the end of the war, two carved wooden cherubs from the top of the Earl Marshal's throne were found to be missing and had to be replaced with newly carved copies. This is one of the few recorded losses among the thousands of objects evacuated to country houses during the war.

Many of the learned societies moved their collections or libraries to the country houses of their patrons. The Royal Zoological Society, for instance, moved its collections to Woburn Abbey, the seat of its president, the Duke of Bedford. The Linnean Society shared the same accommodation in the outbuildings adjoining Henry Holland's Sculpture Gallery. Some of the City livery companies, and Trinity House moved their more valuable treasures to Welbeck Abbey, the seat of the Duke of Portland in Nottinghamshire, where a vast network of underground rooms, executed by the eccentric 5th Duke in the nineteenth century, seemed purpose made for such a function. The Trinity House pictures, nevertheless, came to a sad end. After some time at Welbeck, they were found to be covered with mildew, so were sent back to London to be treated and cleaned. This successfully accomplished, they were stacked in the front hall of Trinity House ready to be taken back to Welbeck the following day. That night, Trinity House received a direct hit by an incendiary bomb and they were burnt to ashes.

On the whole, however, the carefully planned schemes of evacuation of works of art and historical documents evolved before the outbreak of war proved highly successful, and a whole series of country houses was able to provide safe havens for the majority of the nation's art treasures during the worst days of the Blitz. Most of these collections were safely returned home to London in 1945, little the worse for their travels.

Chapter VI
Intelligence

"*Four walls and a roof? Then it's only a C3 billet, at 2d. a night.*"

A small number of country houses situated about an hour's journey north of London, in Oxfordshire, Buckinghamshire and Bedfordshire, played a high security role in the war as headquarters for various of the government intelligence agencies. These included Blenheim Palace (Oxfordshire), Woburn Abbey and Chicksands Priory (Bedfordshire), and Bletchley Park and Hanslope House (Buckinghamshire). Around these major planets were constellations of smaller houses and outbuildings which served as subsidiary offices and accommodation for staff and spies, such as the Old Rectory at Eversholt, Froxfield House and the Paris House, all on the Woburn estate in Bedfordshire. These houses, and the mysterious activities which went on in them, are the origins of those familiar scenes in war films and television serials where a spy or counter-spy is driven down from London to an imposing Palladian house, climbs the steps to a portico, crosses an echoing marble hall and is shown, through a heavy mahogany door, into the room of a cynical man with a moustache who nonchalantly twirls a globe while suggesting some fiendishly complicated, and rather childish, scheme of deception which it is hoped will rock the German High Command to its foundations.

In fact, the houses occupied by intelligence organisations varied in architectural merit. While Blenheim and Woburn were ducal seats and major national monuments, Hanslope was a middling late Georgian house in a Repton park, Chicksands an ancient structure remodelled by Wyatt, and Bletchley a late Victorian house of limited interest surrounded by a sea of Nissen huts. The variety in the scale and style of these houses accurately reflected the character of British intelligence at that time, when it was summed up by an inmate as a disjointed 'jungle of jealous services'.

Much the largest collector of information about other countries was the Foreign Office. The British Foreign Office had existed as an independent department of state since the eighteenth century, Charles James Fox having been the first British Foreign Secretary. In its two centuries of growth and development, it had become one of the best organised in the world, and extremely professional in gathering information about the foreign countries with which it dealt. It was the Foreign Office intelligence section which moved into Woburn in 1939 and established a country headquarters there (CHQ).

British Military Intelligence was more recent (post the 1870 Franco-Prussian War) and also much less organised and efficient than the Foreign Office. During the Second World War, and until relatively recently, there was not a single Ministry of Defence, but three separate ministries each dealing with one of the three service departments, the Admiralty, the War Office and the Air Ministry, all of which viewed each other in a spirit of jealous rivalry. Their tasks were the narrower ones of learning about the size, equipment, organisation and philosophy of foreign fighting forces. They were not staffed by specialists in intelligence, but by ordinary officers on a temporary basis. During the Second World War the RAF had a large photographic intelligence department employed in studying aerial photographs of enemy targets. It was based in two country houses, Nuneham Park near Oxford and Medmenham Abbey in Buckinghamshire. Howard Colvin, the eminent architectural historian, first put his knowledge of buildings to use in this way while in the RAF.

In addition to the departmental intelligence services there was also a number of intelligence activities which made up what is known as 'the Secret Service' (more correctly the Special Intelligence Services or 'SIS'), under a head known as the Chief or 'C', who throughout the war was General Sir Stewart Menzies. The SIS played a leading role in the Second World War by developing cryptographic intelligence and acting as a discreet inter-service agency. In 1939, it established country offices at Hanslope House, Chicksands Priory and Bletchley Park, about fifty miles north of London.

Bletchley Park, or 'BP' as it was familiarly known, is a middle-sized, rambling house of red brick with timbered gables, bay windows and multifarious verandahs and conservatories, rather like an overgrown North Oxford villa. Peter Calvocoressi, who was there during the war, has described it as

more remarkable for its human complement than its architectural dignity. The house had been built shortly before or shortly after the end of the nineteenth century in a style which, up to a few years ago, has been adjudged ridiculous. Even from the more generous quizzical standpoint of today, it is not a striking example of the taste of its times and inside it was dreadful. I remember a lot of heavy wooden panelling enlivened here and there by Alhambresque (Leicester Square, not Granada, Andalusia) decorative fancies. There was a modest stable block and grounds of a few acres laid out as a small park rather than gardens. In a pond in front of the house a few ducks had survived the transfer of the property to government ownership.

The house itself was not large enough to cope with all the staff. Only the 'top brass' were situated there. Everybody else was accommodated in temporary wooden huts erected in the grounds, of which one still survives, 'Hut 3'. Thousands of men and women worked at Bletchley during the war, all concerned with the breaking of codes and ciphers of various grades and in numerous languages, or in appraising and passing on the intelligence discovered from those sources. It is famous as the place where the Germans' most secret wireless code was deciphered and the resulting intelligence assessed. The Germans called their high grade wireless communications 'Enigma' after the machine which enciphered it, and the British called the intelligence derived from it 'Ultra'. Though not a house of great importance, Bletchley neverthe-less made a contribution of crucial importance to the war effort. Peter Calvocoressi, in his book *Top Secret Ultra*, has written:

> The breaking of Enigma ciphers played a signifi-cant part in the Second World War. The value of its contribution varied from time to time and from theatre to theatre, but from the middle of 1940 it

was an ever-present factor. To say that it won the war or even that it won a particular battle would be a silly exaggeration as well as a gross over-simplification of how wars and battles go. But without doubt Ultra made a big difference, sometimes a vital one . . .

The importance of intelligence about the enemy is obvious. To know his strength, his order of battle, his mind – all this is crucial, particularly when he is stronger and winning. There are many ways of getting this information. Most of them involve either intermediaries such as spies of varying dependability, or guessing based on various degrees of insight. But one method is in a class by itself. This is overhearing what the enemy himself is reporting to himself about himself . . .

Ultra was authentic because it consisted of over-heard talk between German commanders them-selves. And it could be unbeatably prompt. In the nature of things a wireless message is intercepted the instant it is transmitted. It is not so easily or immediately deciphered but, given successful cryptographers, it may be read with almost equal celerity. This did not happen all the time or with all high grade ciphers (some of which we never read at all), but we did become used to reading regularly a great many messages between one German unit and another within hours of the time when they were put on the air.

At the end of the war, Bletchley Park was bought by the government in 1947 and retained in service.
Though of greater architectural importance than Bletchley, Blenheim Palace made less of a critical

contribution to wartime intelligence. It served as the offices of MI5 which moved there from Wormwood Scrubs in the London suburbs, after Malvern School moved out of the palace and joined up with Harrow for the last four years of the war. The principal rooms of Blenheim, which had already been adapted for school use, together with a temporary sea of wooden huts in the great forecourt, provided offices for a thousand people. The Marlborough family continued to live in the east wing which formed a self-contained house of its own. Though supposedly highly confidential, the nature of the palace's new occupants was not a very well kept secret. The conductors on the buses from Oxford to Woodstock used to call out in ringing tones when they reached Blenheim's gates, 'Anyone for MI5?'

Woburn Abbey managed to veil itself in a greater degree of secrecy. It was the country headquarters of the Political Intelligence Division of the Foreign Office (CHQ) from the beginning of the war until March 1946. The take-over of Woburn by CHQ is particularly well documented in the Bedford estate papers and makes it a good example to use to chart the change in outlook towards country houses as the war dragged on, from gentlemanly *noblesse oblige* to totalitarian bureaucracy. It also records how attitudes became less civilised and less sympathetic with every year that passed. For this reason, it is worth discussing the Woburn experience at some length.

Woburn became CHQ in the first place because the Duke of Bedford's cousin, Captain Leopold (Leo) Russell (fourth son of Lord Ampthill), was employed in the late 1930s by the Imperial Communications Advisory Committee, then based at Electra House

on the Thames embankment. He had sounded out
the Duke as to the possibility of their moving into
part of the Abbey's vast range of outbuildings in case
of war, and had received a favourable response from
the Duke who had made the Riding School range
available as a military hospital during the First World
War and was anxious to offer that building again as
his personal contribution to the renewed war effort.

The Duke's chief agent, Lt.-Col. E.B. Gordon,
wrote to Leo Russell on 20 April 1939 making a formal offer of various buildings on the Woburn estate
rent free, including Henry Holland's Riding School
and Flitcroft's two spacious stable headquarters, the
Paris House in the park, Froxfield, and the Old Rectory at Eversholt. Five days later, Sir Campbell Stuart
replied with a formal acceptance of the proferred
loan of these properties: 'The government would,
of course, pay for the erection and removal of any
temporary partitions which may be needed and for
the heating, lighting and upkeep of the premises while
occupied by my organisation, and will make good
any damage done.' This exchange of letters initiated
a secret correspondence with Colonel Gordon con-
cerning the detailed plans for the move to Woburn.

In June 1939, work was started on adapting the
buildings to their new use. Partitions were erected in
the Riding School, made of seven foot high wooden
frames covered with Tentact sheeting, to divide the
space into small offices. A new electric mains was
installed to supply the extra lighting and gadgetry
required, the floors were covered over to protect
them and reduce noise, temporary lavatories erected,
acres of blackout material hung in the windows
to meet ARP requirements and concrete air raid

shelters constructed. The initial establishment was planned for 118 people, divided into directing, executive and office personnel, and transport, orderlies and catering staff. The former comprised fifty men and twenty-five women, and the latter twenty-five men and eighteen women. Segregated sleeping space was provided for them, with thirteen principals in Froxfield House and the Old Rectory, thirty-seven men and twenty-five women in the stable bedrooms and another twenty-five men and forty-three women in the loose boxes. The head of the whole operation, Sir Campbell Stuart, was to take up residence in the Paris House in the park (a black and white timbered nineteenth-century 'folly' bought at the Paris Exhibition and re-erected at Woburn); he planned to bring with him his own household staff from London. The others were to be looked after by caretakers and char women recruited locally. As well as the necessary adaptation of the buildings, the miles of private roads in the park were resurfaced to prepare them for the influx of heavier traffic which was expected when the 'emergency' occurred. Woburn was ideally suited to house a secret organisation for not only was the eighteenth-century layout of the house and subsidiary buildings on an enormous scale, almost a small town in itself, but it was secluded at the heart of a vast park surrounded by a high brick wall eleven miles round, designed to keep in the herds of deer and other rare animals, but equally effective in excluding the curious. The various entrance gates were firmly locked and their lodges manned night and day.

Because of the nature of the department which was to occupy the outbuildings at Woburn, all the work was carried out by the Duke of Bedford's estate office at his expense and the cost recovered afterwards from the Foreign Office, so as not to risk disclosure of the identity of the intended wartime occupants. This arrangement, though sensible, worked to the Duke's disadvantage and left plenty of room for quibbling. The estate was in the event to find itself out of pocket as the government balked at paying for re-tarring the drives, claiming that it would have to have been done in any case and was not entirely made necessary by the expected wartime occupation of the place by CHQ. As well as occupying the buildings rent free, thanks to the Duke's generosity, the new offices were also technically exempt from rates and land taxes as government departments do not pay rates. But in order not to damage local authority finances which the massive wartime occupation of private property might have done, the government in this case, and many others, made a 'voluntary contribution' to the local council.

Having himself taken the initiative in offering part of Woburn to the government, the Duke and his agent were at first able to impose their own conditions on their wartime tenants and to secure the inclusion of the following 'General Directions' in the printed orders of conduct:

Everyone is asked to realise that these premises have most generously been put at the disposal of this department by the owner of the estate and that regulations as to the use of the park and buildings have been made to meet with his wishes. The buildings are of historic interest, contain valuable collections of works of art and smoking, therefore, is not permitted anywhere except in the south stable block and even there great care must be exercised.

Any alterations to the buildings required by the Foreign Office had first to be approved by the Duke's agent.

At the end of August, orders were prepared for immediate transfer to Woburn on mobilisation. Detailed instructions were given to the lodge-keepers as to whom they should admit when the time came. Beds were made up in the stables. The rendezvous point for those coming from London was fixed at the Sugar Loaf Hotel at Dunstable, an old coaching inn on the A5. The advance party was planned to arrive at Woburn within six hours of the declaration of war. Despite all this careful planning, the influx when it came was greater than expected and additional accommodation had to be hurriedly prepared. The Duke agreed to add to his original offer a house in the village called Maryland, to increase sleeping space, and the indoor tennis court next to the Riding School for extra offices. The coach houses were also cleared for occupation, all vehicles except the two state coaches and a sedan chair being moved elsewhere. The saddle room, cleaning room and forge were converted into quarters for the men on fire duty, ten of whom were always on stand-by and were fed in the main kitchen of the house. The blackout also proved to be inadequate and an additional 500 yards of black cloth had to be bought quickly in Bedford for 1s.9d. a yard which the agent thought an extortionate price.

Thanks to the generosity of the Duke, and the ready co-operation of his agent and the estate staff, the premises at Woburn were ready immediately on the outbreak of the war for the nucleus of the department which was nicknamed 'the Riding School Organisation' in order to shroud its real nature in decent obscurity. The government, however, had its eye not just on the outbuildings, capacious as they were, and those houses on the estate which had been provided for them, but on the main house as well. There the eighty-year-old Duke lived in solitary state, surrounded by what in 1939 must have seemed immense pomp, huge retinues of servants and quaint eighteenth-century rituals.

On 25 September, the Office of Works wrote to Colonel Gordon: 'The Abbey itself [was] provisionally listed by the Office of Works as unavailable for requisitioning by other departments, or for the reception of evacuees, and I am now instructed to notify you that the Abbey has been definitely earmarked for Sir Campbell Stuart's department alone, as and when the rapidly expanding work of the department necessitates additional accommodation.' Colonel Gordon had already made a gentleman's agreement with Sir Campbell Stuart that the main house would not be requisitioned as long as the Duke lived and that the frail and nearly blind old man would be left in peace to live out his days undisturbed in the Abbey.

On 27 September, Gordon wrote to Campbell: 'With regard to the second paragraph, I hope I understand the situation correctly, and that there is no prospect of the Abbey being occupied by any department as long as the Duke is living there.' In a letter two days later Sir Campbell Stuart confirmed that this was indeed the case.

As a result of this arrangement, the most extraordinary juxtaposition arose, with traditional formal life continuing to revolve around the Duke in the Abbey while the outbuildings teemed with Foreign Office experts engaged in mysterious exercises. In October 'an exceptionally strong wireless loud speaker' and mobile broadcasting apparatus was erected (with the Duke's permission) in the park. And in November, the coach house was converted into a cinema where secret film was carefully studied. The Duke, for his part, was rarely seen, but radiated a distant and feudal benevolence, presenting a football pitch in the park which was 'much appreciated by everyone in the Riding School establishment', arranging through the agent for the officials to be taken on guided tours of the herds of wild animals which he had collected and which roamed freely in the vast grounds: Père David deer, North American bison, wallabies and Highland cattle. At Christmas 1939, the Duke presented the 'Riding School' staff with pheasants, like the rest of his tenants, and allowed them to skate on the ponds in the park.

His own life was extraordinary. In 1939 he still ran the house much as it had been in the nineteenth century, with fifty or sixty indoor servants and the wooden floors washed with beer brewed on the premises for the purpose. Guests were allotted their own personal footman who stood behind their chairs at meals. There was little central heating, except in the corridors, but seventy or eighty wood fires were kept going in the Abbey, even in the bathrooms, throughout the winter. There was electric light, the switches identified with enamel plaques saying 'Electric Light', but a number of candles and oil lamps were still kept ever ready for use in case the new-fangled invention failed. Everything went by the clock. Breakfast was at nine, with individual gold teapots for each person present, lunch at one-thirty and dinner at eight-thirty, on the dot. The Duke had acquired the standards and habits of an ADC in his days in India as a young man in the Victorian vice-regal household and, even at the end of his life, he still attended to every detail of the administration of the house himself, writing short notes or signing chits in black ink, in a firm hand, on scraps usually torn off the backs of used envelopes to save paper. No meal lasted more than half an hour. The Duke at his end of the dining table had a mahogany three-tiered dumb-waiter with plates of radishes and other appetisers which were for him alone and not offered to anyone else. His first course was always beef consommé made in the same way every day, and he drank good claret with ice in it (another habit he had acquired in India). Though not clothes-conscious, he had sixty or seventy similar suits kept, not in cupboards, but spread across trestle tables in four dressing rooms opening off his bedroom.

Conrad Russell, another cousin, stayed with the Duke for Christmas in 1939 and described Woburn as it was then in a letter to Lady Diana Cooper:

> Woburn Abbey, Bletchley
> 23 December 1939
>
> I find Herbrand aged, bent, shrunk, eighty-one and very well. He takes a walk alone every day in all weathers. Lady Ampthill, her daughter Phyllis, Mrs Beaver – sister to Mary Bedford and older.

About seventy-eight and pretty. Quite intelligent. That's all. Diana of course. We sit down six. The cook is good now, very good and came from the Whitbreads (sister to your aunt Lindsay). Dinner is served top speed. I drink claret and all the rest, water. We are out into the Canaletto Room at nine sharp and Herbrand's two nurses are waiting there in tea gowns. They manage the wireless and we all hear the news. After that, chat or pretend to read the papers. At ten-fifteen Herbrand gets up: we all file past him as he stands at the door. The ladies all kiss him. I shake hands. And here I am writing to you. I've got a fine room. Bathroom with a fire burning. My private jakes. I'm very comfortable thank you. There's a Gainsborough in the room, and seven other oil paintings. Most are by Wooten. Dutch perhaps. I've got plenty to read including my grandfather's day book – just been discovered and typed. Foreign travel in 1828.

24 December. A lovely frosty day. Breakfast at nine with rigorous butter economy. Why? And what butter there is and what cream there is much below the Little Clavey's standard. You help yourself to eggs and bacon, the butler takes the plate from you and carries it to your place. You walk behind him. It makes a little procession. As soon as the last person is helped he leaves the room . . .

Herbrand said: 'I don't known Beaufort but I'm sorry for him. I hear he's got Queen Mary in his house. I'm sorry for him poor fella – he's got Queen Mary in his house. Poor Beaufort! It's hard lines on him.' It is indeed.

29 Southwick House, Hampshire. The drawing room in use as the Naval War Room of the Supreme Allied Headquarters. The map on the end wall showing H-Hour on D-Day, 6 June 1944, still exists. Water colour by Barnet Freedman

30 Eaton Hall, Cheshire. Royal Naval College, 1945. 'The
    Quarter Deck'

31 Eaton Hall, Cheshire. Royal Naval College. The
Common Room

32 Eaton Hall, Cheshire. Royal Naval College. Cadets
preparing boats for a race on the River Dee in the park

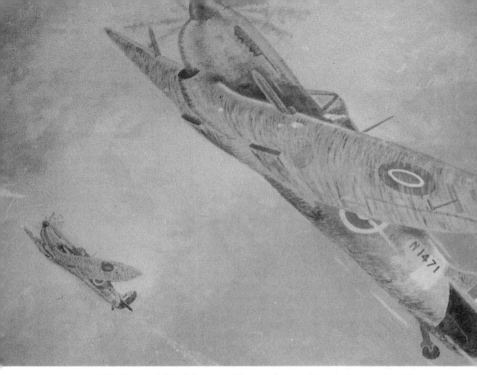

33 Ramridge House, Hampshire. A spitfire painted on a
bathroom wall by Flying Officer W. T. Orr, 1944

34 Markeaton Hall, Derbyshire. Military graffiti in the
Music Room showing Churchill and Adenauer

35 The North Court of Harlaxton Manor, Lincolnshire, showing Pegasus badge of the 1st British Airborne Division which occupied the house during the Second World War

36 Felix Hall, Essex. Burnt, January 1940

37 Shillinglee Park, Sussex. Gutted by fire during a party
held by Canadian troops in 1943

38 Beaurepaire Park, Hampshire. Burnt and demolished,
1942

39 Melford Hall, Suffolk. East wing gutted by fire, March 1943

40 Newton Ferrers, Cornwall. Damaged by fire, 1940

41 Mount Edgecumbe, Cornwall. Gutted by incendiary bombs, 1941

42 Egginton Hall, Derbyshire. Demolished 1954, after the interior was wrecked by military occupation in the Second World War

Woburn Abbey, Bletchley
Christmas 1939

I've had one Xmas present today and given one. I
received a view of Woburn Abbey from Margaret
at breakfast. And I gave Herbrand a cheese. The
presentation was made at two pm when he came
into the Canaletto Room for luncheon. I think it
was a success, but it was unexpected and so long
since he had been given a present that he hardly
knew what to say. But he was pleased in his
way I do believe. I didn't go to church. After
breakfast D and I went into Woburn town and
called on Andrews my yeomanry Sergt; we had
a crack or chinwag as I noticed Mrs Andrews
called it. Then we strolled about and looked at
the ornamental water fowl. One of Herbrand's
nurses came to luncheon and her presence made it
somewhat more animated. Then we all listened to
the King's broadcast and I thought the impediment
in his speech was worse than ever. After that, walk
in the grounds and feed the duck and geese on the
Chinese Dairy pond and get lost in the maze. Tea
and read *Escape*. Then to my room and wrote to
Maurice and Goonie. It's a pretty queer sort of life.

A queerness here is when one comes out of
the dining room into the Canaletto Room there's
a servant waiting for us standing in the Canaletto
Room. He bows low to Lady Ampthill and Herbrand and then shuts the dining room door. He's
posted there for that I suppose – to shut the door.

I asked Marjorie [Russell] how many different
messes were served below stairs and she didn't
know at all. But once when she went to the kitchen
she saw about fifteen men in blue serge suits (not

footmen) whom she's never seen before. There are only two men in livery – those in evening clothes are all called 'Mr So and So'. There seem to be four of this rank. There's also a male housekeeper who doesn't wait.

While all this was going on, the officials in the Riding School, many of whom were socialists, were beginning to get impatient of waiting for the Duke to die. In May 1940 they started to make serious efforts to move into the Abbey. Colonel Gordon wrote in response: 'The Duke is naturally anxious not to have a host of officials and clerks quartered in the Abbey.' He was ill and nearly blind, and felt he had done everything that could reasonably be expected. Gordon added for good measure, and with some truth, that the government's needs were extravagant. The estate had done all their building work for them and a clerk of works was kept fully employed seeing to their needs, the Duke bearing this extra cost. When the officials began to rattle the dread threat of compulsory requisitioning, Gordon played his trump card, Sir Campbell Stuart's written confirmation that his department would not occupy the Abbey as long as the Duke lived. He also enlisted the help of a friend, Alan Lennox-Boyd, then the Minister of Food, 'in these times when minor officials have such powers, against which there is no appeal (as they delight in pointing out!) . . .' Colonel Gordon prevailed and the plans to invade the Abbey itself were dropped for the time being.

But this proved a temporary respite. The Duke of Bedford died on 27 August 1940 and was buried in

the Russell family vault at Chenies in Buckinghamshire after a funeral service at Woburn to which the
King sent an official representative. The estate staff
dispatched letters in black-edged mourning envelopes
embossed with the head of Edward VII and bought
in bulk at the beginning of the century.

The feudal time-warp at the Abbey was extin-
guished immediately after the Duke's death. The
'Age of Hooper' had arrived. In the same month, Sir
Campbell Stuart was replaced as head of the 'Riding
School Department' by Rex Leeper. The new Duke,
a man of cranky views with well-publicised pacifist
and even pro-Hitler outlook, was considered a security risk and was not allowed anywhere near Woburn
by the authorities. He spent the war at his shooting
lodge in Scotland, Cairnsmore near Wigton, but sent
to the Abbey his formidable factotum, Mrs Osborne
Samuel, to protect his interests. Extremely grand in a
large car with a chauffeur, she immediately proceeded
to ruffle everybody's feelings with a series of brusque
missives written in green ink which were a far remove
from the gentlemanly reasonableness of the *ancien
régime* at Woburn. Her note to the chief agent on 26
October 1940 provoked his immediate resignation:

> Dear Colonel Gordon, I shall be glad if you will
> leave the government officials to me. Any plans
> or information given to them must be given by
> me. It is perhaps unfortunate, but I am the official
> servant of the Duke here, and hope to do my duty.
> Therefore will you please respect this . . .

He was succeeded by William Higgs. On 7 November 1940, the whole of the Abbey was requisitioned

compulsorily with the exception of the Plate Room and Muniment Room. The estate was also allowed to retain the libraries in the south wing for the storage of the paintings and more valuable furniture. The 'non-valuable' furniture was requisitioned with the building. Christies were employed to sort out the contents, supervise the storage arrangements, and devise suitable insurance policies. Wooden huts to provide additional offices were built in the forecourt between the entrance portico of the Abbey and the stables. The CHQ now took over completely, and the number of officials crammed into the Abbey and outbuildings rose to several hundred. Anybody admitted through the lodge gates was compelled to sign the Official Secrets Act. Top Secret dispatch boxes rattled up and down from the Foreign Office on a daily basis. Hordes of brilliant young men, including Dick Crossman, worked away.

Sefton Delmer, an Australian-born journalist who was employed for a time by CHQ as director of 'Black Operations' gives some idea of what they were all up to in the second volume of his autobiography, *Black Boomerang*. One of their functions was to collect information to be used in radio broadcasts to Germany, intended to mislead and break the morale of German civilians and troops. 'German Soldiers' Radio Calais' which made continental broadcasts in German was not based at Calais nor was it German. It was a British counterfeit German broadcast aimed at causing confusion among the enemy and giving instructions to foreign resistance groups. It was not entirely unconnected with the 'exceptionally strong wireless loud speaker' in the park at Woburn. The reports of spies and other sources, even the contents of the daily German newspapers were collected in the Riding School and perused for facts which could be built up into misleading stories. From time to time, leading figures at the Foreign Office, Lord Vansittart, Valentine Williams, Hugh Dalton and Leonard Ingrams, would descend on Woburn to take part in interminable meetings to decide what CHQ should do, for example when Germany attacked Russia.

After 1943, as the tide of the war began to turn, the establishment at Woburn began to run down and much of it was moved back to London. In August that year, CHQ retreated once more to the Riding School block, and the emptied Abbey was re-allocated for the billeting of Wrens (WRNS) till the end of the war. During all the time that the buildings were occupied, no proper maintenance was carried out, with the result that there were severe outbreaks of dry rot which spread rapidly through the largely timber structure of Henry Holland's Riding School and tennis court. By March 1946, when the Abbey was de-requisitioned, most of the buildings were empty and decaying. Towards the end there were only six people left there. The new Duke, on returning to Woburn from Scotland, was so appalled by the condition of the place, that he decided to demolish half of it, but died in a shooting accident before he could complete the work of reduction and renovation. The present Duke, who inherited in 1953, records his impression of Woburn after the ravages of wartime occupation and his father's misguided efforts to deal with the problem:

My first visit to Woburn in thirteen years was a

shattering experience. I had not been there since my grandfather's death and no member of the family had lived there in all that time. When my father returned from Scotland after the war, he lived in one of the houses in the village, while the reconstruction work he had ordered was put in train. As the long drive from the lodge gates curved round the last wooded hillock I gasped. The Abbey looked as if a bomb had fallen on it. The building which had housed the indoor riding school and the tennis court, connecting the two Flitcroft stable blocks, had disappeared; so had the whole of the east front, together with at least a third of the north and south wings where it had joined them. There were piles of stones and building materials lying in a haphazard fashion all over the place, and the courtyard in the centre of the house was full of Nissen huts. There were one or two workmen around, but otherwise the place was deserted. A troop of Alsatian dogs, chained to long wires, kept watch at most of the gates, and you could hear them barking and their chains rattling like some eerie scene out of *The Hound of the Baskervilles*.

The interior was freezing cold and desolate. It looked as if it belonged to a series of bankrupt auction rooms. There were piles and piles of linen baskets in the front hall, right up to the ceiling, and mounds of furniture lying everywhere, most of it without dust sheets. There were beautiful Louis XV chairs with kitchen-table legs straight through the seat; the walls and cornices were peeling and everything was covered in dust, and filthy. The whole house reeked of damp. It looked as if no general maintenance work had been done at all. I do not think my father had paid any attention whatsoever to the details of upkeep, and after one quick tour I despaired of ever breathing life into the place again.

In fact the Duke did not despair but restored the Abbey and its contents to their old glory, and opened the place to the public on a commercial scale, transforming it into a major tourist attraction, thus ensuring its future.

Chapter VII
The Armed Forces

"Yes, you can tell them back in Oregon that you're staying at a typical English country seat."

The lion's share of the large country houses requisitioned during the war was taken by the armed services for a wide variety of uses from billets, supply-bases and officers' messes to strategic, signals' and training headquarters. Many houses were occupied by successive waves of different military organisations and fighting men of different nationalities. Some of these treated the buildings better than others, but from the point of view of the owners, occupation of their houses by the armed forces, especially by the army, was the worst fate that could befall them. Clough Williams-Ellis, the Welsh architect, wrote of military occupation as the final 'indignity of so many large country mansions, where their last tenants, our own British army, too often reduced them to virtual ruin'. Troops were often rough, and vented their high spirits, or ill-feelings, on the fabric of the house. Much damage, however, was not so much caused by deliberate vandalism – though there was enough of that – but resulted from attempts to make an inadequately prepared structure habitable and, in particular, to provide some heating. Thus wooden fittings tended to be chopped up for fuel, and large fires banked up in small fireplaces with unswept chimneys often had disastrous results. More will be said about the resulting damage in the next chapter.

Conditions in many requisitioned houses were

poor. Evelyn Waugh dismissed with a few acerbic words a typical set-up at Kingsdown House, Kent, where he found himself billeted in January 1940. The house was derelict and 'surrounded by little asbestos huts . . . one bath for sixty men, one wash basin, the WCs all frozen up and those inside the house without seats. Carpetless, noisy and cold. A ping-pong table makes one room uninhabitable, a radio the other. We are five in a bedroom without a coat peg between us.'

Many country houses in 1939 were only habitable if staffed by large numbers of domestic servants to keep the fires going and to carry hot water to where it was needed. Most large English houses at that time had very little central heating, and a woefully inadequate supply of bathrooms. Without servants and endless log fires, they were icy cold and lacked even the basic facilities of a purpose-built Victorian barracks. To call the typical country house 'an uncomfortable great barracks of a place' was to do an injustice to barracks. It is not surprising therefore that the armed forces were often less than enchanted to find themselves billeted in an Adam mansion with no running water.

There is only space here to describe a representative sample of the thousands of country houses of all shapes and sizes occupied by the armed services during the Second World War. When the war broke out, the service departments did not at first envisage anything like the scale of requisitioning that in the event took place when the conflict escalated and military arrangements on the home front mushroomed. As events unrolled, more and more houses were taken over to meet particular emergencies. In the early days of hostilities, the emphasis was on acquiring houses and estates which could be used for training purposes as the army was expanded to full war-footing by the call-up of reservists and volunteers. Many properties in the south-west were requisitioned for tank training, out of the reach of German bombing raids, including Tyneham, parts of Lulworth, Smedmore and Crichel Down, all in Dorset. The British Expeditionary Force was assembled, for the same reason, in Wiltshire, Somerset and Dorset and made its last-minute preparations there, prior to crossing over to France. The troops were billeted in temporary camps and a variety of buildings, including stables and cottages, while the officers' mess or battalion headquarters were often set up in the big house of the district. Wilton House became the headquarters of Southern Command, Amesbury Abbey was used for billeting troops, Longford Castle was used for billeting and its grounds for camouflage training. Large military camps were erected near Stourhead and in the park of Dinton House. Much of this provided a hasty expansion of the army's ordinary training camps on Salisbury Plain. In the north, a similar rapid expansion of facilities for the military took place around the army camp at Catterick, especially to the west in Westmoreland where moors were requisitioned for training on either side of the A66 road. Lowther Castle was used for billeting troops and smaller country houses like Warcop Hall were transformed into officers' messes.

The requisitioning of houses by the army was done by the quartering commandants of different regiments. The War Office also employed its own land-agents to deal with the owners and to settle the financial details, negotiating payments in lieu of rent for occupation of property and compensation for damage. Philip Miles, a captain in the army, was one of fourteen land-agents in West Sussex employed by the War Office to deal with claims and to work out agreements with the owners of houses which were being requisitioned. He spent four and a half years in the job, and recalls in particular the pressure to find accommodation for the British troops evacuated to the south coast after Dunkirk. At that time Parham Park in Sussex, the property of Clive Pearson, was requisitioned by the quartering commandant, and Captain Miles had to settle the arrangements with the owner. Parham was the most famous Elizabethan house in Sussex and had been carefully restored and modernised by the Pearsons in the 1930s. Unlike the majority of large English country houses, it was very comfortable and had central heating and plenty of bathrooms. The Pearsons were agreeable to having their house requisitioned, but asked for the oak panelling and other features of historic interest to be adequately protected. As it was an Elizabethan house, the Office of Works agreed to do this, and the Chief Inspector of Ancient Monuments was sent down to advise on the precautions to be taken to safeguard the building. Not all the house-owners in Sussex were as co-operative as Clive Pearson. Lingfield Manor, for instance, had to be taken by force and the owner, an angry woman, locked in the kitchen.

Following the collapse of France in 1940 and the rapid evacuation of the British Expeditionary Force, accommodation had to be found at short notice for a sudden influx of 300,000 troops. During 1940, the War Office greatly expanded the numbers of country houses which it occupied in all parts of the country. In the face of the threat of invasion there was a large build-up of the British Army with the training of new recruits and the formation of new regiments and battalions. By 1941, there were over two million troops (British and Colonial) based in England, Scotland and Northern Ireland, many of them in country houses. To take random examples in different parts of the country: the 6th Battalion the Leicestershire Regiment was at Ashby St Ledgers in Northamptonshire, the Lutyens-designed house of Lord Wimborne; the 11th Battalion the Green Howards was at Seaton Delaval, Vanbrugh's masterpiece on the Northumberland coast; the 70th Battalion East Surrey Regiment was at Capel Manor in Kent, a Victorian Gothic pile by Thomas Henry Wyatt. The 11th Battalion Worcestershire Regiment was at Haselbech Hall in Northamptonshire, an Edwardian Jacobean house belonging to the Ismay family (of the Shipping Line). This was a new regiment raised on Hereford Race Course in February 1940. A.R. Kibblethwaite who was posted to it in October 1940 remembers Haselbech:

> In the middle of December of that year we moved into Northamptonshire as Lorried Infantry to the 9th Armoured Division, Bn. HQ being Haselbech Hall, the residence of Mrs Constance Ismay, widow of Bower Ismay of the Cunard Line (*Titanic*) fame, Mrs Ismay having moved into the cottage opposite the Hall. Although in her seventies, she was the most hospitable person I ever met, both officers and troops having the greatest affection for her.

A company was also billeted in Lamport Hall, the

house of the Ishams. Another company was at Highfield House, Husbands Bosworth (now knocked down), and another at The Hemplow, just outside Welford. The Carrier Platoon and medical officer were billeted in a house in that village.

The division had great promise, having one or two crack regiments – the North Irish Horse and the Enniskillen Cherry Pickers among them – and the division sign was a panda. The regiment was based at Haselbech for two years, and after they left American forces took their place in the house. Mrs Ismay was comfortable in the cottage in the village where she spent the war. James Lees-Milne, her nephew, visited in January 1942 and recorded the snug, if somewhat Heath-Robinson, arrangements:

> I continued to Haselbech for the night, where I found Aunt Con in her new cottage, which is too technological for words, being fitted from top to bottom with electrical gadgets. You press one button beside the bed, and a metal arm offers you a cigarette in a cardboard holder; another, tea spouts from a tap into a cup; yet another and the mattress becomes as hot as St Lawrence's gridiron . . . The whole room was a tangle of wires inadequately insulated. I was in terror of being electrocuted.

The troops in the big house were faced with less cosy arrangements.

The largest of all English country houses, Wentworth Woodhouse, the seat of Earl Fitzwilliam near Sheffield in Yorkshire, was used for a variety of military purposes throughout the war, beginning as a battalion headquarters for various regiments in the

Northern Command and ending up as the Intelligence Corps depot. The Fitzwilliam family remained in residence throughout the war, the house being enormous enough to contain both them and a regiment. As in the case of Woburn Abbey, the history of Wentworth Woodhouse in these years charts a decline in civilised standards. At the beginning of the war the family retained the major part of the house, including all the superb eighteenth-century state rooms in the main block. Lord Fitzwilliam acted as host to his wartime tenants who were billeted in the side wings and stables, giving parties for them, presenting them with bottles from his cellar and allowing them to use his billiard table. By the end of the war, the Fitzwilliams were in retreat, occupying only a portion of the south front, the state rooms were being knocked about by troops, the furniture and paintings stacked in heaps, and the park and gardens compulsorily open-cast mined to the detriment of Repton's planting and the destruction of some of the eighteenth-century temples which embellished them.

Dr Patrick Hewlings, who was posted to Wentworth Woodhouse in 1940, after the British Expeditionary Force was evacuated from France, recalls the atmosphere in the house then:

My posting was as Regimental Medical Officer to the 10th Battalion, the Duke of Wellington's Regiment. This was a new battalion being formed, and when I arrived at Wentworth Woodhouse I found only a 'skeleton' Battalion HQ and HQ Company staff. Gradually more staff and many new recruits arrived, the latter mostly Yorkshire miners still in mufti and their traditional 'flat caps'. Our job was to train these chaps as quickly as possible as infantry soldiers, and transform them into an active fighting unit. Only Battalion HQ and the HQ Company were accommodated in Wentworth Woodhouse. The other four companies were billeted in the surrounding country – I remember that one company was in Barnsley . . .

If you stand facing the front elevation of the house, my recollection (after forty-eight years!) is that there was a stable block and a long wing on the right hand of the main building and another long wing – possibly servants' quarters – on the left hand. The Earl and Countess Fitzwilliam lived in the central block of the house, and I think they retained all of the main part for themselves. The 'other ranks' – i.e. 'the licentious soldiery' – were billeted in the stable block: the officers (and possibly the sergeants) were quartered in the wings of the house. We were very comfortable. We had use of his Lordship's billiard table. Lord Fitzwilliam visited our mess, usually on Sunday morning before lunch and had a drink with us. He liked a little 'military gossip'. He had served in the Army himself when younger and he very often brought a bottle of his excellent port as a present to our mess for consumption after Sunday dinner.

Lady Fitzwilliam was also very hospitable and asked some of the wives – camp followers – to tea. She also introduced her very beautiful granddaughter, Lady Diana Montagu-Stuart-Wortley, the daughter of the Earl of Wharncliffe, to some of the officers, and she caused quite a flutter in the dovecote! But although some subalterns cherished faint hopes, she later became Duchess of Newcastle!

And Lady Fitzwilliam gave a 'ball' – I think it must have been at Christmas 1940 – to the officers in the Saloon, with its marble floor on the first floor, a memorable occasion.

On the whole, it was a very happy billet. The Fitzwilliams were very good to us, and I don't think they were much incommoded by the military presence.

Later, Wentworth Woodhouse was taken over by the Intelligence Corps depot. Brian Fothergill, the writer, was billeted there in April 1945 before being posted to the Japanese theatre of war and found himself in Carr of York's massive quadrangular stable block, reputedly built out of the winnings on the turf of Whistlejacket, the famous eighteenth-century racehorse owned by Lord Fitzwilliam's ancestor. He wrote to his mother on 11 April: 'We *are* billeted in the stables, but they are very nice as stables go.' A few days later, he added:

There is very little here to write about – life is reduced to routine and each day is the same as the last. However, it is nice living in this delightful park – even if we do sleep in the stables. Lord Fitzwilliam still lives at Wentworth Woodhouse, but has been banished from the main part and probably has to content himself with a small suite of a hundred rooms or so. There are supposed to be 365 windows in the house, but I have never had leisure to count them myself.

By that time, Lord Fitzwilliam was no longer dispensing port, and the house itself was in a state of crisis with 'the army creating havoc within and open cast mining encroaching from without'. Soon afterwards, the family moved away and most of the house was let after the war for educational use, the great eighteenth-century state rooms never reinstated and their contents scattered.

The West Country continued to be particularly favoured by the military after Dunkirk. The Grenadier Guards for instance, re-grouped in Somerset and Wiltshire for further training, including tank training on Salisbury Plain in preparation for the North African and Italian campaigns. They were based at a series of country houses, including Marston in Somerset, the seat of the Earls of Cork and Orrery, Red Lynch in Wiltshire, a house of the Earls of Suffolk and Berkshire, and Stourhead, where they occupied the cellars and a nearby temporary camp. Conrad Russell noted in July 1940 that the 1st Battalion Grenadier Guards were at Marston 'where the Corks lived. I hope they'll stay. It gives one a sense of security.' By August, they had moved to Nunney, but Russell kept in touch with them. (There were family connections, his brother Gilbert had fought with the Grenadiers at Omdurman). In between military routine they helped him on his farm at Mells:

I've seen Miles Howard [the present Duke of Norfolk] now Adjutant, 1st Batt Grenadier Guards at Nunney about two miles away. To my surprise, we are buddies. He will send Grenadiers to help my harvest whenever I like. 'How many can you send?' I said. And he said: 'Will eight hundred do?'

And Russell dined with them in their mess:

> The whole evening was a Wow. It is the war
> as I remember it. Bovril in tin mugs, a good
> mixed dish of tongue, bacon, duck and sausage,
> coffee in tin mugs and port in celluloid tumblers.
> A semi-ruined cottage – candles guttering. Bear
> was next the CO and I was next the second-
> in-command (Major Llewylln). We sat a long,
> long time and I listened breathless while Major
> fought his battles o'r again: 'This is Govt's HQ
> (the salt cellar) – Belgian HQ was here (a mus-
> tard pot) – this is the Meuse where those
> buggers let 'em through (an empty bottle of
> port)', etc. etc. I sat spellbound. When we broke
> up it was a lovers' parting: 'You'll come again?'
> 'Yes, yes, of course.' 'And you'll come and see
> us at Stourhead?'

James Lees-Milne encountered them at Stourhead
while he was negotiating with the Hoare family for
the transfer of the house to the National Trust. He
found soldiers billeted in the basement of the house,
and the Guards Brigade Headquarters nearby. The
current unit was just about to leave and during
breakfast the officers of the departing unit came
in one by one and 'fervently thanked the Hoares
for their kindness, and expressed genuine sorrow to
be going. Lady Hoare is much exerted. The Hoares
are in their eighties, a charming old couple living
on their memory of their son killed in the First
War.'

In many cases the greater part of the regiment was
billeted in small houses and cottages, farm buildings,

stables, or under canvas, with the mess and battalion headquarters only in the big house. Wilton House, for example, was not used for billeting troops but was Southern Command Headquarters throughout the war, the Double Cube Room being used for meetings, and much of the planning for the D-Day landing was prepared there. The Earl and Countess of Pembroke continued to live in the house, mainly in Wyatt's Library on the west front. Like Lord Fitzwilliam in the early days of the war at Wentworth Woodhouse, they performed their duty and acted as hosts in their own house to the occupying military, being included in group photographs with the commanding officers, and presiding over garden parties in the grounds, including one on Independence Day in July each year for American officers based in Wiltshire.

There was a large influx of American troops into England from the summer of 1942 onwards, preparatory to the opening of the Second Front. They were decanted into country houses in all parts of Britain, often displacing evacuated children who in turn were packed off back to the cities whence they came, or sometimes replacing British soldiers. The headquarters of General Patton and the American Third Army was at Peover Hall near Knutsford in Cheshire, a Jacobean house, then with a large Georgian wing which was reduced to such a state that it was demolished after the war and the house returned to its original Jacobean dimensions. Sunninghill Park in Berkshire (the site of the Duke and Duchess of York's new house) was used as a training base by American service men. They left behind in the lake, when they departed, an armoured jeep, at least one hundred shells and other live ammunition, all of which were discovered during dredging operations in September 1988.

At Arundel Castle in Sussex, American troops were billeted in the east range of the quadrangle, and three thousand acres of Downland on the estate, including the Duke of Norfolk's new racing stables and gallops, were temporarily requisitioned for tank-training. The south tower of the castle served as a look-out post, part of the Channel Coast defences. When the castle was rebuilt as a Victorian evocation of mid-thirteenth-century Gothic by the 15th Duke of Norfolk in the 1870s, neither he nor his architect, Charles Alban Buckler, can have envisaged that less than a century later their machicolations, arrow slits and drawbridges would have to serve a military role as part of the wartime defences of England. The 16th Duke of Norfolk and his family lived in the castle throughout the war, mainly in the Smoking Room on the ground floor of the main block which was converted into an all-purpose living room with a dining table, library of racing books, deep armchairs and a billiard table moved from elsewhere; it remains much as it was then and is still the cosiest room in the castle. The furniture and paintings from the east wing and the state rooms were stored in the vast Barons' Hall, a room 150 feet long on the west side of the quadrangle. One chilly antiquated bathroom, untouched since its installation in 1906, was kept out of bounds to troops and reserved for the use of WAAFs from the nearby Ford airfield. A faded notice from the door reads: 'This bathroom is for the use of WAAFs only.'

Many families stayed on in a portion of their houses alongside the military occupation of the other rooms or wings. At Holkham in Norfolk, for instance, the 3rd Earl of Leicester remained in the house throughout the war, living in the family rooms on the west side. The state rooms on the *piano nobile* of the central block were kept under dust covers, while the east side of the house, including the kitchen wing, stables, skittles alley and a large range of outbuildings, as well as various farms on the estate, were occupied by the army which used the reclaimed marshland and sand dunes along the coast for training. The numbers and names of tanks – *Anson, Atlas, Albatross, Albacore* and *Albemarle* – can still be read in faded paint above their parking spaces on the wall of the kitchen court. That of Albemarle is particularly appropriate as the second wife of 'Coke of Norfolk', 1st Earl of Leicester, was a daughter of the 4th Earl of Albemarle. The Coke family assumed that Holkham, so close to the coast and the German Ocean, would be in the front line when the invasion came. When asked what he would do to repulse the German Army, the elderly Earl replied that he 'would call out the keepers in case of an invasion'. He assumed that the Nazis would occupy the house as a headquarters and dreaded the prospect as 'unlike the Kaiser, Hitler [who was 'not a gent'] would *never understand houses*'. Melodramatic plans were conceived for local activists to blow up the Marble Hall as the Nazi officials marched up the Grand Staircase. Lord Leicester, who had served in Egypt in 1882, Suakin in 1885 and in the Boer War, remarked that every 'man, woman and child in Norfolk is looking forward to killing at least two Germans'. He was disappointed by Hitler's attack on Russia 'as now the invasion is definitely ORF, and everybody likes a bit of campainin'.'

Holkham was not to play a glorious last role in the front line after all. The house and its treasures survived the war unscathed, though some of the estate buildings were left derelict (Model Farm is being properly restored only at the time of writing) and the practice-shelling of the sand dunes weakened the sea-defences. This caused tidal flooding of several low-lying farms thus enabling the estate to lodge a substantial claim for compensation against the War Office which proved a very useful source of capital for modernising the farms in the financially straitened years after the war.

As well as British and American troops, there was a wide range of continental and commonwealth troops based in country houses. Some houses hosted a whole succession. Deene Park in Northamptonshire, for instance, was 'invaded' by successive waves of Czech, Polish and Indian soldiers, as well as British. The Free French were also based in Northampton-shire at Finedon Hall, the seat of Major Greaves who moved to a cottage in the village, but kept a close eye on the Hall. James Lees-Milne visited in January 1942 and found the big house unfurnished: 'at present [it] houses Free French troops. They were most off-hand and rude to the poor Major, who I could see was a great tribulation to them, constantly prowling around and extolling his own property. They kept crabbing it in front of him . . .' Black troops provided a Firbankian touch in several houses, including, most appropriately, Faringdon House in Berkshire, the seat of the composer-writer-painter-aesthete, Lord Berners, the original of Nancy Mitford's Lord Merlin. The troops occupied the upper floors of the house while Lord Berners and his

friend Robert Heber-Percy, as well as Robert's wife
Jennifer and baby, lived downstairs in the principal
rooms. The whole set-up must have been among
the most curious of many curious wartime country
house ménages, an effect enhanced by Lord Berners'
taste for colouring the white pigeons in the garden
in various bright tints. James Lees-Milne found the
place

> attractively untidy in an Irish way, with beds, but
> beautiful ones, scattered in the downstairs rooms.
> Much confusion and comfort combined. Jennifer's
> baby Victoria playing on the floor of the kitchen
> like a kitten. Lord Berners said that this afternoon
> one of the negro soldiers – and the place is stiff
> with them – accosted him in the garden with the
> request: 'Massa, may I pick just a little bunch of
> flowers for our Colonel?'

There were regional variations in the concentration of troops. The Canadians, for instance, seem
mainly to have been in the south, Kent, Sussex
and Hampshire. Wakehurst Place in Surrey served
for two years, from 27 January 1942 to 23 October
1943, as the headquarters for the Canadian Armed
Forces under the direction of General Crevar. The
Canadians were given, at that time, the responsibility
for forward line defence of the Sussex coast in case of
a German invasion. The dog kennels at Wakehurst
were converted into an underground signals station
to control the movement of troops. Large temporary
camps for the Canadian soldiers were established on
several Sussex estates, including the great avenue at
Stansted Park, the seat of the Earl of Bessborough,

where it was hoped that the trees would help camouflage the settlement from the air, and in 'Capability' Brown's superb park at Petworth where again the eighteenth-century disposition of clumps of beech trees and oaks helped to provide cover. Later, the Canadians were concentrated in the southern counties prior to the ill-fated Dieppe raid. Many were billeted in the small country houses in which the region abounded, such as the Old Manor House at Hartley Wintney in Hampshire, a Victorianised early seventeenth-century, half-timbered house, which was occupied by three Canadian regiments in succession, including the Cameron Highlanders of Ottawa, the South Saskatchewan Regiment and the Elgin Regiment of Canada.

The RAF and the USAAF were also to an extent regionalised, with a heavy concentration in eastern England from Yorkshire down to Essex, and to the north-west of London along an axis from Uxbridge to High Wycombe in Buckinghamshire. Of course there were airfields and billets in western England, too, in places where the land was flat enough; for example, at Fazackerly north of Liverpool and around Preston on the Lancashire coastal plain. Eastern England being less hilly than the west, and nearer to the enemy, however, was the main scene of the great building programme of new airfields which took place in the 1930s and throughout the war. Most of these were provided with purpose-built accommodation for the airmen and ground personnel, but neighbouring houses were in many cases taken over to serve as the officers' mess or as offices for senior officers. At Bradwell on the Blackwater estuary in Essex, for instance, the local RAF fighter station requisitioned Bradwell Lodge, the eighteenth-century house of Tom Driberg, the MP, to serve as its officers' mess.

In Norfolk, several country houses were occupied by the RAF, including Blickling Hall, the first fully-fledged property of the National Trust which removed most of the furniture and paintings for safe-keeping to another part of the country. James Lees-Milne was responsible, as the Trust's historic buildings secretary, for the property and paid several visits in the course of the war.

Moving up the east side of the country, Harlaxton Manor in Lincolnshire was requisitioned as the headquarters of 1st Airborne Division. The owner, Mrs Van der Elst (the daughter of a Middlesex coal porter and a Quaker washer-woman, who possessed a large fortune derived from the manufacture of Shavex) was confined, against her will, to a few rooms. The Airborne Division left behind a memorial of their occupation of the house in the form of a tablet depicting their Pegasus insignia, in the north courtyard. Another, different sort of memorial is the record of the occupation by Bomber Command Number One Group of Bawtry Hall (subsequently demolished) near Doncaster. It was the subject of one of the very few colour films shot during the Second World War, and it is fascinating to see the eighteenth-century architecture contrasting with various 'black boxes', charts and map tables of the RAF. The film, shot by Air Commodore Henry Cozens, is still available (Thorn-EMI).

The air forces seem to have left behind them more acceptable memorials of their stay in country houses than the other services, and several have been preserved down to the present day by the owners of the houses in question. At Redhayes, near Exeter, an Edwardian house requisitioned for use by both the RAF and the USAAF in connection with Exeter airport, one wall of the main bedroom is wholly taken up by a huge map of northern Europe extending from Exeter to Berlin. At Ramridge House near Andover in Hampshire, the wall of a ground floor room is still embellished with a fine mural (dated 1944) of a spitfire painted by Flying Officer W.R. Orr during the time that the house was an RAF headquarters and the room was used as an officers' mess.

The major concentration of air force-requisitioned houses was in south Buckinghamshire and north Middlesex. RAF Bomber Command was at Naphill, High Wycombe and Sir Arthur 'Bomber' Harris, and Sir Charles (later Lord) Portal had offices there. The USAAF headquarters in Britain from 1942 to 1945 was at Wycombe Abbey, a Wyatt Gothic house formerly a seat of the Marquess of Lincolnshire, now a girls' school. Hughenden Manor, also near High Wycombe, Disraeli's old home and a property of the National Trust, was taken over by an RAF Signals Station. Bentley Priory in Middlesex, another Wyatt house, was the headquarters of Fighter Command and the office of Lord Dowding. Sir Francis Dashwood recalls that West Wycombe Park became a regular venue for many of the senior RAF officers in the district, and those of the American 8th Air Force, who frequently dropped in for a nutritious Sunday luncheon of roast rabbit or teal in aspic. West Wycombe was hospitable in more ways than one to the surrounding forces. At the end of the war the Dashwoods found scribbled in chalk on the kitchen wall in the hand of the scullery maid: 'Boys. Olive is here.'

Though not strictly occupation by the services, the wartime role of Salisbury Hall near St Albans is worth mentioning. This seventeenth-century, moated manor house with Nell Gwynne associations was rented by Captain Geoffrey De Havilland in 1938 for developing his own idea for a versatile aeroplane made of wood. After the Air Ministry had scornfully turned down the project, he decided to go it alone at his own expense. Therefore, the Mosquito was designed and the prototype built at Salisbury Hall, screened from prying eyes by the moat. The first Mosquito was flown out of the next-door field. It is a marvellous story of private determination triumphing over blinkered official indifference and has been written by R.E. Bishop in his book *The Wooden Wonder*.

The largest concentration of naval-occupied country houses was situated, not surprisingly, in the south and especially the Hampshire hinterland of Portsmouth, many establishments being hurriedly transferred to the country following the bombing of the Royal Dockyard in spring 1941. The regional headquarters of the Admiralty at Bath was housed mainly in hotels, schools and the spa buildings, rather than country houses. Apart from the numerous houses used for billeting the WRNS, a small group of larger mansions played a key role as Royal Navy training establishments, including Foots Cray, Kent, an eighteenth-century English version of the Villa Rotunda, taken over by HMS Worcester in 1940, Laydene House, near Petersfield, taken over at the beginning of the war by HMS Mercury, the Royal Naval Signals School, and Eaton Hall in Cheshire, the

Victorian Gothic palace of the Dukes of Westminster, occupied for a time by the Royal Naval College from Dartmouth.

The most important of all was Southwick House in Hampshire. This early Victorian stuccoed mansion, looking like a straggler from Belgrave Square, was taken over in 1941 by HMS Dryad, the Navigation School, a refugee from the bomb-wrecked Portsmouth dockyard. In 1943, however, it became the operations centre for the Supreme Allied Commander, General Dwight Eisenhower, and also the headquarters for Admiral Ramsay, the Naval Commander-in-Chief. In 1944, the main house was sealed off from the rest of HMS Dryad and, amidst the greatest security, plans were formulated there for the allied invasion of Europe. The drawing room was converted into the headquarters room of the Allied Expeditionary Force, one wall being covered with the invasion map which formed part of a larger map of Great Britain and the whole European coastline from North Norway to the Spanish frontier, provided by a toy firm in the Midlands. When the map arrived at Southwick House, the section required for the Normandy landings was separated from the remainder and erected in the drawing room. To maintain further secrecy, the two workmen and the naval officer who erected it were required to remain in the house till the invasion of Normandy was under way. The map remains *in situ*, having been preserved as a memorial at the end of the war, and shows H-Hour in the British sector on 6 June 1944. As Supreme Allied Headquarters and the place where the invasion of Normandy was planned and controlled, Southwick perhaps played the most prominent role of any of the country houses occupied by the armed services in the Second World War. From there, Eisenhower issued his noble exhortation on the eve of the invasion to the three million men taking part in the Allied Expeditionary Force:

> Soldiers, sailors and airmen of the Allied Expeditionary Force:
>
> You are about to embark upon the Great Crusade, toward which we have striven these many months. The eyes of the world are upon you. The hopes and prayers of liberty-loving people everywhere march with you. In company with our brave allies and brothers-in-arms on other fronts, you will bring about the destruction of the German war machine, the elimination of Nazi tyranny over the oppressed peoples of Europe, and security for ourselves in a free world . . .
>
> Good Luck: and let us all beseech the blessing of Almighty God upon this great and noble undertaking.

There was also a substantial naval concentration in Scotland, Pitreavie Castle in Fife, for instance, serving as a maritime headquarters for the naval bases in the Firth of Forth, and the major Combined Operations bases were scattered all along the west coast of Dunbartonshire, Argyll and Inverness-shire, the seashore there being considered safest from enemy bombardment. A whole series of houses and castles were requisitioned. Inverailort House on Loch Ailort, the seat of the Cameron-Head family was used for training 'combined ops' RNVR officers. Rosneath Castle, a neo-classical house built by the

5th Duke of Argyll to the design of Bonomi, became HMS Rosneath; Glenfinnan House HMS Armadillo; Tullichewan Castle was transformed into WRNS quarters; and Inverary Castle, the seat of the Duke of Argyll, became the centre of a vast encampment, Loch Fyne covered with ships, and the hills crawling with service manoeuvres. The Duke, an expert in church ritual and Saxon coins, remained in residence surrounded by a sea of hutments. James Lees-Milne who visited in September 1943 noted an amusing and characteristic incident. A conscientious soldier on duty tried to stop the Duke from walking up one of the wooded rides in the park and received the reply: 'What's this? I can go where I like. I am the Duke.'

Chapter VIII

Damage and Destruction

" *Austria, Czechoslovakia, Poland. And now, dammit, Hunting.*"

The damage caused by troops during the Second World War is part of the folklore of the English country house. Nearly every house which was used to accommodate the military has some horror story to retail of staircases chopped up for firewood, subsidiary wings gutted, the Van Dycks used as dartboards, jeeps driven through wrought iron gates or stone balustrades, carved or painted graffiti, smashed windows and much else besides. Allowing for some exaggeration and the inevitable embellishment of stories over the years, there is a good deal of truth in this particular wartime myth. Troops did cause terrible damage to many country houses, hundreds of which were never privately occupied again after 1945. A substantial number were demolished as a direct result of wartime damage, including Gopsal and Garendon in Leicestershire, Egginton in Derbyshire, Sudbourne and Redgrave in Suffolk, Easton in Lincolnshire, Warnford Park in Hampshire, Rufford Abbey in Nottinghamshire and Methley Hall in Yorkshire.

Others, like Woodfold Park and Clayton Hall in Lancashire or Rigmaden Park and Lowther Castle in Westmorland, were simply abandoned by their owners who could not face them again after military occupation; and this resulted in some bizarre situations. At Baron Hill on the Isle of Anglesey the house of the Bulkeley-Williams family remained as it was when vacated by troops at the end of the war till its demolition *circa* 1980. In the 1970s, the interior, though in the last stages of disintegration, still sported chalked military notices on the walls, and rotting Christmas decorations left over from the last winter of the war still festooned the collapsing ceilings.

A small number of English country houses were accidentally damaged or destroyed as a direct result of enemy action. Appuldurcombe, the eighteenth-century baroque house of the Worsleys on the Isle of Wight, which had been quietly decaying for several years between the wars, was finally wrecked by a landmine falling in the park, and is now just a shell in the guardianship of English Heritage. At Hellens, Much Marcle, Herefordshire, a romantic brick house of ancient date, a stray bomb intended for Birmingham fell on the courtyard in 1940, demolishing various later accretions, but leaving the original building standing. Swainston on the Isle of Wight, a part medieval, part late Georgian house of the Simeon baronets, was gutted by an incendiary bomb in 1941, though it was restored after the war at great cost. Other houses had their windows blown out by bombs falling in the park, including the Manor House at Mells in Somerset, Deene Park in Northamptonshire, Knole in Kent, and Castle Bromwich Hall near Birmingham where all the sixteenth-century heraldic glass was smashed by a nearby blast.

The major country house victim of aerial bombardment was Mount Edgecumbe in Cornwall, the important mid-sixteenth-century seat of the Earls of Mount Edgecumbe, situated in a beautiful park on a promontory in Plymouth harbour. It was completely gutted by incendiary bombs in 1940, the Germans having mistaken it for a fortification of the naval dockyard. Only part of the shell and the four polygonal corner turrets of the Elizabethan house survived, though the interior was subsequently rebuilt to the design of Adrian Gilbert Scott at the expense of the War Damage Commission, the official body set up by the government to compensate owners for the destruction of their property as a result of enemy action. Such damage was not, of course, covered by ordinary insurance policies.

The other major country house accidentally destroyed by bombing in the Second World War was Sandling Park in Kent. This was a neo-classical house, designed by Joseph Bonomi for William Deedes in 1799. It received a direct hit during a bombing raid on London in 1943, and the ruined shell was demolished in 1945.

Enemy action was responsible for a very small fraction of the damage caused to the English country house. Far more houses were destroyed by their British or Allied occupants than by German bombing. It was generally agreed that soldiers were the worst possible occupants of fragile historic buildings. James Lees-Milne recorded laconically of Stoke Ferry Hall in Norfolk in February 1944: 'The soldiery just left – therefore the condition is deplorable.' Though the military must accept the lion's share of the blame, no wartime occupation of a house was entirely risk-free. As already seen, Castle Howard was seriously damaged by fire while tenanted by a girls' school. Marks Hall in Essex, the house of the Gilbey family, was burnt by the land girls stationed there smoking in bed.

Evelyn Waugh gives more detail of the usual treatment in the epilogue to *Brideshead Revisited*:

'Wonderful old place in its way,' said the Quartering Commandant; 'pity to knock it about too much . . .

'Now this is where the last lot put the clerks; plenty of room, anyway. I've had the walls and fireplaces boarded up you see – valuable old work underneath. Hullo, someone seems to have been making a beast of himself here; destructive beggars, soldiers are! Lucky we spotted it, or it would have been charged to you chaps . . . Very decent fellows the last lot. They shouldn't have done that to the fireplace though. How did they manage it? Looks solid enough. I wonder if it can be mended?

'I expect the brigadier will take this for his office; the last did. It's got a lot of painting that can't be moved, done on the walls. As you see, I've covered it up as best I can, but soldiers get through anything – as the brigadier's done in the corner. There was another painted room, outside under pillars – modern work but, if you ask me, the prettiest in the place; it was the signal office and they made absolute hay of it; rather a shame.

'This eyesore is what they used as the mess; that's why I didn't cover it up; not that it would matter much if it did get damaged; always reminds me of one of the costlier knocking-shops, you know – "*Maison Japonaise*" . . .

'That fountain is rather a tender spot with our landlady; the young officers used to lark about in it on guest nights and it was looking a bit the worse for wear, so I wired it in and turned the water off. Looks a bit untidy now; all the drivers throw their cigarette ends and the remains of the sandwiches there, and you can't get to it to clean it up, since I put the wire round it. Florid great thing, isn't it? . . .'

Starting at the top of the scale of destruction, a not insubstantial number of houses were either burnt down entirely, or at least partly gutted by fire. Even when not burnt, damage was often caused to the interior decorations by smoke. The library in the Evelyn house at Wooton in Surrey was completely blackened by fires piled up too high in the grate, and the Adam rooms at Mersham le Hatch in Kent were similarly begrimed. Any pieces of furniture left *in situ* were used as firewood, including mahogany shelves from bookcases or drawers from chests. At Shugborough in Staffordshire, where a large military encampment was established at the south end of the park, the classical park temples designed by 'Athenian' Stuart in the mid-eighteenth century were much knocked about, and the U-shaped table inside the Tower of the Winds, used by the 1st Earl of Lichfield for gambling parties, was chopped up and burnt for kindling.

Every county can show examples of houses burnt down by troops in the 1940s. In Berkshire, Arborfield and Clewer Park were both set on fire and demolished in 1943. In Cornwall, Newton Ferrers was partly burnt in 1940. In Cumberland, Brayton Hall, the huge Georgian mansion of the Lawsons, was totally destroyed by fire in 1940. In Devon, Clovelly Court was largely damaged by fire in 1944 and Shobrooke destroyed entirely. In Dorset, the Down House was burnt in 1941. In Essex, classical Felix Hall was gutted in 1940 and Gothick Belmont Castle burnt and the shell demolished in 1944. In Hampshire, Beaurepaire Park, a romantic old Tudor House, was burnt and demolished in 1942, and West Park in 1945. In Hertfordshire, Newsells Park, a seventeenth-century house of the De Trafford family was burnt in 1943. In Kent, North Cray, a version of Palladio's Villa Rotonda was burnt in 1945. In Leicestershire, Edmondthorpe was set on fire by troops in 1942 and reduced to a shell. In Lincolnshire, Harpswell fell victim to the flames in 1944; in Norfolk, Watlington Hall, an early nineteenth-century pile by Donthorne went up in smoke in 1943; in Suffolk, Carlton Hall was completely destroyed by fire in 1941, and one wing of the Hyde-Parkers' Tudor mansion at Melford Hall gutted, though later subsequently restored. In Sussex, the major portion of Shillinglee Park was gutted by Canadian troops in 1943 and left a shell for the best part of thirty years. In Warwickshire, Oldbury Hall was destroyed by fire in 1941 and in Wiltshire, the nineteenth-century wing of Longford Castle was damaged by fire and demolished after the war. Lea Castle in the same county succumbed in 1945, and in Yorkshire, Sunderlandwick Hall, an early Victorian house in the East Riding, was burnt down by the RAF during celebrations on VJ night in 1945. In Scotland, Loudon Castle, Ayrshire, a vast Gothic pile designed by Archibald Elliott in 1811, was incinerated in 1943 and Dalmeny, the early nineteenth-century, Tudor-revival house designed by William Wilkins for the Earl of Rosebery was part gutted by the RAF but subsequently rebuilt.

Fire was a major hazard not just for the main house, but also for the decorative outbuildings in the park of a country house. At Slindon in Sussex, the little Regency temple with an ironwork Trafalgar balcony round the outside was burnt out by the troops stationed on the estate. Some of these fires were caused by over-enthusiastic attempts to keep warm and overloaded chimneys, but others were caused by glowing cigarette ends. The Second World War coincided with the widest social incidence of smoking in England. Nearly the whole population, men and women, smoked nearly the whole time. Casually discarded cigarettes were lethal when combined with the ancient dust, dry woodwork and straw insulation of old houses. During the war, as at other times with country house fires, there was never enough water to dowse the flames, especially in winter when any decorative ponds in the grounds were likely to be frozen solid.

At the other extreme from fire was flood. Many houses were seriously damaged by dry rot caused by burst pipes, leaking roofs and blocked gutters, all hazards in ill-maintained and inadequately heated buildings. James Lees-Milne describes a typical example in April 1945 when he visited Slebach, the Welsh house of Sheila de Rutzen:

. . .a delightful house. A fresh unit of troops was trying to clean up the appalling mess left by the last. Since January, water has been allowed to seep from the burst pipes through the ceilings and down the walls. Most of the stair balusters have disappeared. Mahogany doors have been kicked to pieces. Floor boards are ripped up. All rooms mottled with and stinking of damp. I imagine dry rot has set in everywhere.

At Egginton Hall in Derbyshire, the troops left all the taps running when they left in 1945. By the time this was discovered the interior was waterlogged and several of the Wyatt ceilings had collapsed. The owner decided there was nothing to be done but to demolish the house and to move into the stables.

Sheer neglect was as much responsible for the ruination of houses as positive ill-treatment. Six years' intermission in routine maintenance with no roof repairs or painting of window frames was in itself enough in the damp English climate to cause serious problems. At Woburn Abbey, for instance, it was purely lack of proper maintenance and heating which caused massive outbreaks of dry rot and led to the demolition of nearly half the buildings after the war. It was particularly dispiriting for owners who had spent a lot of money on repairing their property before the war to find all their efforts wasted and that they had to start almost from scratch.

At Rigmaden Park in Westmorland, a Greek-Revival house designed by the Websters of Kendal, the Wilsons, who own it, had re-done the roof during the 1930s. Occupation by troops during the war and neglect of the gutters led to new outbreaks of dry rot. They decided to cut their losses and abandon the place. It remains today a crumbling shell in a jungle of undergrowth, though the present owner is seriously considering re-roofing it.

Troops usually managed to ill-treat a building even if they did not burn it to the ground or flood it. Mary, Duchess of Buccleuch, recalls the wartime occupation of her husband's various Scottish houses:

War came, oddly enough, before one expected it. The army moved into Bowhill with not a thing put away. The officers' sitting room was where all the Van Dycks were. It was terribly badly used; the army did terrible things to the house, all the proverbial things that troops are supposed to do – hacking down the banisters to make firewood, and throwing darts at the pictures. They couldn't have done more harm, and ended up by nearly burning it down twice. But it survived . . . Bowhill was a barracks; Drumlanrig was a school; and the other houses were also barracks. Langholm had to be pulled down after the war – it couldn't be shored up, because it had got such dry rot in it, through the troops being there for four and a half years.

Many stories of destruction are difficult to prove. At Marston House in Somerset, for instance, one branch of the double plan cantilevered stone staircase in the Great Hall, designed in 1858, collapsed during the wartime military occupation of the house. One explanation is that it did so while a company of Grenadier guardsmen were marching up it. The other, more irresistible, legend is that it fell down later in the war when the house was occupied by American troops. They used the wide shallow-rising stone stairs to race their jeeps up one flight of steps, along the landing and down the other flight, till one day the treads gave way and the whole of the right-hand branch of the staircase collapsed on to the Great Hall floor. The most elaborate version of this story adds a few fatal casualties.

Whether the staircase at Marston was demolished by a jeep race or not must remain speculative. But there is no doubt that damage was done to many other architectural features by racing jeeps or other military vehicles. At Compton Verney in Warwickshire, the stone balustrade of Adam's elegant bridge over 'Capability' Brown's lake was knocked over by a recklessly driven vehicle. A favourite ploy was to drive straight through a pair of closed iron gates at speed. The gates designed by Samuel Wyatt at the main entrance to Doddington Hall in Cheshire met their end in this way. Though the owner was compensated for the damage, he spent the money on new farm buildings rather than replacing the gates which remain missing to this day. At Amesbury Abbey in Wiltshire, the troops billeted in the house managed to smash not just the entrance gates, but demolished one of John Webb's flanking gate piers as well. On the whole, however, country houses were too remote for the government to bother removing all the ironwork for scrap in the way that led to the loss of most of the old architectural ironwork in London and other cities. Only a few houses situated near to the capital suffered in this way. For instance, the Victorian iron gates at the entrance to West Wycombe Park were commandeered in 1942.

It is arguable whether English or foreign and commonwealth troops were the most destructive. Canadian soldiers would seem on occasion to have been particularly troublesome. Those billeted at Dunorlen Park near Tunbridge Wells in Kent cut the heads off all the statues in the garden one night. At Brocket in Hertfordshire they carved their names, addresses and numbers inches deep into the balustrade of James Paine's bridge in the park. James Lees-Milne, while regretting this piece of vandalism, added in his diary, 'Yet I thought what an interesting memorial this will be thought in years to come and quite traditional – like the German mercenaries' names scrawled in 1530 on the Palazzo Ducale in Urbino.'

The Free Czech troops stationed at Port Lympne, the former home of Sir Philip Sassoon in Kent, wreaked havoc on that fastidious connoisseur's 'Rothschild-Levantine' decorations and totally destroyed the famous elephant paintings by Sert in the drawing room which were the finest example of 1920s Parisian decorative art in England. Italian prisoners of war at Rufford Abbey in Nottinghamshire tore down all the silk brocade hangings to make into handbags for their girl friends. At Greystoke Castle in Cumberland, Polish soldiers, as well as running an illicit still in an old lime kiln, did so much damage to the late eighteenth-century Gothick wing that it had to be demolished after the war. At Kedleston, American troops unscrewed and stole the ormolu rosettes from the centre of the Adam-designed door handles in the state rooms as souvenirs, and at Alton Towers in Staffordshire, the Gothic wonderland created by the Earls of Shrewsbury, they machine-gunned the conservatories one particularly boisterous evening.

James Lees-Milne's record of his perambulations of the country on behalf of the National Trust in the years between 1942 and 1945, provides many authentic instances of the damage caused to country houses by their wartime occupants. In May 1942, he noted at Jacobean Blickling in Norfolk, by that time the property of the National Trust, that the RAF had needlessly broken several casement windows and smashed the old Crown glass, and forced the locks of the doors to the state rooms out of devilry:

'This sort of thing is inevitable.' A more serious incident occurred later when they used a tree-trunk battering ram to force open the heavy door of Bonomi's pyramidal eighteenth-century mausoleum in the park, and broke into the marble sarcophagus of the Countess of Buckinghamshire to see if there was any jewellery inside. On another visit he wrote: 'It is a sad, lonely, unloved house with a reproachful air. I dare say it will be burnt down before long.'

Privately-owned houses he found in an even worse state than National Trust property. In June 1942, he visited Culverthorpe in Lincolnshire 'in deplorable condition owing to the troops stationed there'. The splendid hall had been partitioned into an orderly room and officers' mess, the capitals of the columns boarded up and the painted panels shrouded in canvas. Haudoroy's frescoed ceiling over the staircase had a great crack in it, several windows were broken and a stove had blackened the stonework. At Netley Park in Surrey in January 1943, he recorded that the 'licentious soldiery had made an awful mess' of the main rooms, including smashing the pair of gilt-framed looking glasses over the fireplaces in the drawing room. At Coleshill in Berkshire, Sir Roger Pratt's masterpiece, he noted in April 1943 that part of a wall to the service court, including one of the magnificent seventeenth-century gate piers, had been blown up in an accidental explosion by the troops in part occupation of the house. Similar incidents were to be encountered all over the country.

By the end of the war in 1945 most country houses had reached the nadir of decay, dirty, battered, ill-maintained for six years, even when not the object of more conspicuous damage. Frequently, irreplaceable schemes of historic decoration had been painted out with a healthy coat of cream paint. At Elton Hall, the seat of the Proby family near Peterborough, the rich Victorian colour scheme in the State Dining Room was distempered over. At Carlton Towers in Yorkshire the flock wallpapers designed by J.F. Bentley in the bedrooms were all colour-washed, and the even more splendid paper on the walls of the dining room removed altogether. Once such old schemes of decoration had been painted over, it proved impossible to restore them. For the average country house owner in 1945, his property must have posed a seemingly insoluble problem. Apart from the deplorable condition of the interior, the grounds were often an overgrown jungle and the estate derelict.

The attitude of house owners in 1945 to their lot varies. Some were furious at the damage caused to their property. Most were resigned, even stoical. James Lees-Milne who visited Winstanley Hall near Wigan in Lancashire, the home of 'Squire Bankes', in June 1945, recorded an instance of the latter:

> The park is open-cast mined. The ATS have occupied half the house. The whole place is devastation. It has broken the old man's heart and he can talk of nothing else. Yet he shows no bitterness.

Some owners gave up the unequal struggle before it had begun and simply abandoned their houses. Nearly a thousand country houses were demolished in Britain in the ten years between 1945 and 1955, largely as a result of damage caused during their wartime occupation. Some like Lowther Castle in Westmorland were reduced to shells so as to serve as landscape features, or follies, in the park while the owner moved to a smaller house nearby, whereas others such as Rosneath Castle in Dunbartonshire were blown up with dynamite. Several houses, including Woburn, Knowsley, Brocklesby and Aske were drastically reduced in size to make them more manageable. Another group of houses were given to the National Trust to secure their preservation. The largest portion of houses, however, were restored as family homes after the war and their owners moved back, often opening them to the public as well. Government policies were part helpful, part unhelpful. By continuing wartime rationing of building materials and restricting all building work for years after the end of the war, they made it difficult for owners to do the necessary works of repair and adaptation till it was too late. While compensation was paid through the War Damage Commission to repair buildings, the amounts of money given paid no recognition to the need to meet the costs of re-adapting the houses to their old residential use under new social conditions with much reduced domestic staffs and straitened economic circumstances. Only the institution of historic buildings grants in the 1950s and the revival of English agriculture provided many landowners with the financial wherewithal to pay for the restoration and adaptation of their houses from the mid-1950s onwards.

A serious immediate threat to the country house at the end of the war was the fear of compulsory purchase. Under the Requisitioned Land and War Works Act 1945 (8 & 9 Geo. 6 c.43), the government gave itself the power compulsorily to purchase houses which had been adapted to a wartime use, regardless of the wishes of the old owner or assurances given in 1939. By this means, several country houses were retained for public use in 1945. Trent Park, near Barnet, the main house of Sir Philip Sassoon, was compulsorily acquired at the end of the war for educational use. Southwick Park in Hampshire was retained by the Admiralty against the wishes of its owner, and continues to serve as HMS Dryad today.

Ralph Dutton, whose house Hinton Ampner was considered for acquisition by the Royal Observatory, has described what it felt like to be threatened by the public authorities at that time. In April 1945 his land agent received a letter announcing that a party from the service departments headed by the Astronomer Royal would be visiting Hinton on the 16th of that month in order to inspect it with a view to taking it as a site for the new Royal Observatory. He was horrified. After six years of war and centralised bureaucratic control, the service departments had total autocratic power against which there was no appeal. He decided that the best thing was to meet the officials and to talk to them on the spot. He was still employed by the Foreign Office, but he managed to take the day off and was standing on his own doorstep when the party of twenty or so arrived. He gave vent to his feelings, explaining how the house had been in his family for centuries and how much it meant to him; to lose it would be worse than the amputation of a limb. The officials were slightly embarrassed but showed no sign of being dissuaded from their nefarious purpose. Some time later, however, a short, somewhat casual note arrived announcing that they had decided against Hinton Ampner and taken Hurstmonceaux Castle in Sussex instead. It was not till 1953 and the Crichel Down débâcle, when Major Allington successfully retrieved part of the Crichel estate which had been taken for tank training, that the tyranny of the service departments was defeated and landowners began to feel relatively secure again. In the case of Hinton Ampner, Ralph Dutton was able to move back in in 1945. The girls' school which had been in occupation of the house did not return after the Easter holidays, but went back to their own premises in Portsmouth. Compared to many houses, Hinton came through the war relatively unscathed. The furniture stored in the stables was affected by damp, and that stacked in the library was eaten by moth. The whole place needed redecoration, and some of the walls were enlivened with childish graffiti declaring that 'Miss So-and-So was a So-and-So'. Though superficially dilapidated, the place was basically sound. The school paid a small sum for dilapidations, and gradually over the years the house was put right as fast as building licences and black-market decorators allowed.

The amazing thing after 1945 is not that so many country houses were given up and demolished in the aftermath of the Second World War as that the majority were restored and revived. Attitudes to houses depended partly on generations. The older owners could not envisage returning to their houses in changed circumstances and without substantial domestic help. The younger generation was more energetic and determined to make a go of it. Having won the war, they were not going to be daunted by dry rot and collapsing ceilings. Relying largely on their own labour and the judicious use of second-hand furnishings or army surplus, they brought derelict historic interiors back to life.

Annette Bagot remembers how she and her husband, Robin, moved into Levens Hall in Westmorland after the war. Between 1939 and 1945 it had been occupied by the nuns from Roehampton Convent in London on the recommendation of Catholic neighbours, the Hornyold-Stricklands of Sizergh Castle. The nuns had treated the house well, but all the carpets, which had been rolled up and stored, had been eaten by moths, and all the upholstery and curtains were worn out. The chairs looked more as if covered with cotton wool and dirty tatters rather than silk brocade. The Bagots decided to restore the house, live in it and open it to the public – only the garden had been open before the war. Their professional advisers tried to dissuade them, saying that it was impossible to live in the place with an income of less than £5,000 a year. They had less than half that, but managed to make do. They found a number of second-hand carpets of the right size in Liverpool, salvaged from old ocean liners. At first there was no staff and Mrs Bagot did all the cleaning, polishing the panelling and woodwork. Gradually, they got the place into shape, with five or six gardeners to look after the famous topiary and a team of indoor dailies.

The same story can be repeated of many other houses which were revived after the war thanks to the devotion and hard work of their owners. Despite everything, the largest portion of English country houses survived the war and in the subsequent forty years or so have been restored to their old state. As long ago as 1960, Evelyn Waugh admitted that *Brideshead Revisited* was a premature epitaph, a panegyric preached over an empty coffin.

Appendix

An Act to provide for compensation in respect of action taken on behalf of His Majesty in the exercise of certain emergency powers; and for purposes connected with the matter aforesaid.

[1 September 1939]

2 and 3 Geo.6

Be it enacted by the King's most Excellent Majesty, by and with the advice and consent of the Lords Spiritual and Temporal, and Commons, in this present Parliament assembled, and by the authority of the same, as follows:

Right to, and measure of, compensation

1 (1) Where, in the exercise of emergency powers during the period beginning with the twenty-fourth day of August, nineteen hundred and thirty-nine, and ending with such day as His Majesty may by Order in Council declare to be the day on which the emergency came to an end,

- (a) possession of any land has been taken on behalf of His Majesty, or
- (b) any property other than land has been requisitioned or acquired on behalf of His Majesty, or
- (c) any work has been done on any land on behalf of His Majesty, otherwise than by way of measures taken to avoid the spreading of the consequences of damage caused by war operations,

then, subject to the following provisions of this Act, compensation assessed in accordance with those provisions shall be paid, out of moneys provided by Parliament, in respect of the taking possession of the land, the requisition or acquisition of the property, or the doing of the work, as the case may be . . .

2 (1) The compensation payable under this Act in respect of the taking possession of any land shall be the aggregate of the following sums, that is to say,

- (a) a sum equal to the rent which might reasonably be expected to be payable by a tenant on occupation of the land, during the period for which possession of the land is retained in the exercise of emergency powers, under a lease granted immediately before the beginning of that period, whereby the tenant understood to pay all usual tenant's rates and taxes and to bear the cost of the repairs and insurance and the other expenses, if any, necessary to maintain the land in a state to command that rent, and

(b) a sum equal to the cost of making good any damage to the land which may have occurred during the period for which possession thereof is so retained (except in so far as the damage has been made good during that period by a person acting on behalf of His Majesty, no account being taken of fair wear and tear or of damage caused by war operations, and

(c) in a case where the land is agricultural land, a sum equal to the amount (if any) which might reasonably have been expected to be payable in addition to rent by an incoming tenant, in respect of things previously done for the purpose of the cultivation of the land, and in respect of seeds, tillages, growing crops and other similar matters, under a lease of the land granted immediately before possession thereof was taken in the exercise of emergency powers, and

(d) a sum equal to the amount of any expenses reasonably incurred, otherwise than on behalf of His Majesty, for the purpose of compliance with any directions given on behalf of His Majesty in connection with the taking possession of the land:

Provided that

(i) in computing for the purposes of paragraph (a) of this subsection the rent which might reasonably be expected to be payable in respect of any land, and in computing for the purposes of paragraph (c) of this subsection any amount which might reasonably have been expected to be payable in addition to rent by an incoming tenant, no account shall be taken of any appreciation of values due to the emergency; and

(ii) there shall not, by virtue of paragraph (b) of this subsection, be payable in respect of damage to any land a sum greater than the value of the land at the time when possession thereof was taken in the exercise of emergency powers, no account being taken of any appreciation in the value thereof due to the emergency.

(2) Any subsection under paragraph (a) of the preceding sub-section shall be considered as accruing due from day to day during the period for which the possession of the land is taken in the exercise of emergency powers, and be apportionable in respect of time accordingly, and shall be paid to the person who for the time being would be entitled to occupy the land but for the fact that possession thereof is retained in the exercise of such powers; but this subsection shall not operate so as to require the making of payments at intervals of less than three months.

For the purposes of the enactments relating to income tax and the enactments relating to land tax, and in particular for the purposes of such of those enactments as relate to the deduction of tax from rent, any compensation under the said paragraph (a) shall be deemed to be rent payable for the land, the Crown shall be deemed to pay it as tenant occupier, and the person receiving it shall be deemed to receive it as landlord.

(3) Any compensation under paragraph (b) of subsection (1) of this section shall accrue due at the end of the period for which possession of the land is retained in the exercise of emergency powers, and shall be paid to the person who is then the owner of the land.

(4) Any compensation under paragraph (c) of subsection (1) of this section shall accrue due at the time when possession of the land is taken in the exercise of emergency powers, and shall be paid to the person who, immediately before that time, was the occupier of the land.

(5) Any compensation under paragraph (d) of subsection (1) of this section shall accrue due at the time when the expenses in respect of which the compensation is payable are incurred, and shall be paid to the person by whom or on whose behalf those expenses were incurred.

3 (1) Compensation under this Act in respect of the doing of any work on any land shall be payable only if the annual value of the land is diminished by reason of the doing of the work.

(2) The compensation payable under this Act in respect of the doing of any work on any land shall, in the first instance, be a sum calculated by reference to the diminution of the annual value of the land ascribable to the doing of the work, and shall be paid in instalments, quarterly in arrear, to the person who for the time being is entitled to occupy the land.

Any compensation under this subsection shall be considered as accruing due from day to day, and shall be apportionable in respect of time accordingly.

(3) If, at any time after compensation under the preceding subsection has become payable by reason of the doing of any work on any land, a person acting on behalf of His Majesty,

(a) causes the land to be restored, so far as practicable, to the condition in which it would be but for the doing of the work, or

(b) serves on the person for the time being entitled to occupy the land a written notice of intention to discharge the liability for the compensation by making, not earlier than a date specified in the notice, payment of a lump sum in accordance with the following provisions of this section,

the period in respect of which compensation is payable under the preceding subsection by reason of the doing of the work shall end with the date immediately preceding the date on which the restoration is completed or, as the case may be, the date specified in the notice.

(4) Where, by virtue of the operation of the last preceding subsection in relation to any work done on any land, the period in respect of which compensation under subsection (1) of this section is payable by reason of the doing of the work comes to an end, then if, at the expiration of that period, the value of any estate or interest which a person then has in the land is less than it would be but for the doing of the work, there shall be paid to him, by way of compensation under this Act, a sum equal to the amount of the said depreciation in the value of the estate or interest; and that compensation shall be taken to accrue due at the expiration of the said period.

(5) As soon as may be after effecting any restoration or serving any notice in pursuance of subsection (3) of this section, the person by whom the restoration was effected or the notice was served shall cause the fact of the restoration or the contents of the notice, as the case may be, to be published in such manner as he thinks best adapted for informing persons affected.

(6) In determining for the purposes of this section whether the annual value of any land is diminished by reason of the doing of any work thereon, and in assessing any compensation under this section in respect of the doing of any work on any land, it shall be assumed that the land cannot be restored to the condition in which it would be but for the doing of the work.

(7) For the purpose of this section, no account shall be taken of any diminution or depreciation in value ascribable only to loss of pleasure or amenity.

(8) No compensation under this section shall, in relation to any land, be payable in respect of any period for which possession of that land is taken on behalf of His Majesty in the exercise of emergency powers.

(9) In this section,

(a) the expression 'annual value' means, in relation to any land, the rent at which the land might reasonably be expected to let from year to year, if the tenant undertook to pay all usual tenant's rates and taxes and to bear the costs of the repairs and insurance and the other expenses, if any, necessary to maintain the land in a state to command that rent; and

(b) the expression 'diminution of the annual value' means, in relation to the doing of any work on any land, the amount by which the annual value of the land is less than it would be if the work had not been done . . .

Index

Acton family, 58-9
Admiralty, 6, 12, 53, 108, 150, 171
Air Ministry, 8, 12, 13-14, 95, 108, 150
Air Raid Precautions Act, 6
Airborne Division, 1st, 148
Aldenham, Shropshire, 58-9
Allington, Major, 172
Alton Towers, Staffordshire, 167
American 8th Air Force, 149
American Third Army, 142
American troops, 28, 136, 142-3, 167
Amesbury Abbey, Wiltshire, 133, 166
Ampthill, Lady, 119, 121
Anderson Committee, 22
Appleton Hall, 29
Appuldurcombe, Isle of Wight, 158
Arborfield, Berkshire, 161
Argyll, 5th Duke of, 153
Armoured Division, 9th, 135-6
Arundel Castle, Sussex, 143
Ascott, Buckinghamshire, 100
Ashby St Ledgers, 135
Ashridge, Hertfordshire, 79
Aylmer, Mrs, 53-7

Badminton, Gloucestershire, 29-37
Bagot, Annette and Robin, 173
Baillie, Lady, 73
Baldwin, Stanley, 21
Bangor University, 96
Barnardo Homes, 22, 27-8
Baron Hill, Anglesey, 157-8
Bath, Marquess of, 52-3, 54, 57-8
Battlesden Abbey, Bedfordshire, 80
Bawtry Hall, near Doncaster, 148
Beaufort family, 29-34, 36, 37, 120
Beaumont, Lady, 73, 76, 77
Beaurepaire Park, Hampshire, 162
Bedford, Dukes of, 12, 15, 17-18, 22,
    104, 112-13, 115-23, 125-7
Belmont Castle, Essex, 162
Belvoir Castle, Leicestershire, 101
Bentley, J. F., 76, 169
Bentley Priory, Middlesex, 149
Berners, Lord, 145-6

Berwick, Lady, 16
Bessborough, Earl of, 146
Bishop, R.E., 150
Blakiston, Noel and family, 101
Blenheim Palace, Oxfordshire, 63-6,
    107-8, 111-12
Bletchley Park (BP), 14, 107, 108,
    109-11
Blickling Hall, Norfolk, 86, 148, 167-8
Board of Education, 6, 13
Bonomi, Joseph, 153, 159, 168
Boughton, Northamptonshire, 99
Bowhill, Scotland, 165
Bradfield Park, Berkshire, 79
Bradwell Lodge, Essex, 147-8
Brayton Hall, Cumberland, 161-2
Bristol, bombing of, 34; evacuees, 27
British Legion, 95
British Military Intelligence, 108-9
British Museum, 94, 99, 102
Brocket, Lord, 80
Brocket, Hertfordshire, 80, 166-7
Brown, Lancelot 'Capability', 147,
    166
Bryanston School, 64
Buccleuch, Duke of, 99
Buccleuch, Mary, Duchess of, 164
Buckingham Palace, 93, 98
Buckinghamshire, Countess of, 168
Buckler, Charles Alban, 143
Bulkeley-Williams family, 158

Caernarvon Castle, 96
Calvocoressi, Peter, 109-11
Cameron Highlanders of Ottawa, 147
Camperdown Prep School, 66-70
Canadian troops, 146-7, 162, 166
Canford School, 64
Capel Manor, Kent, 135
Capesthorne, Cheshire, 79
Carlisle, Earl of, 63
Carlton Hall, Suffolk, 162
Carlton Towers, Yorkshire, 73, 76-7,
    169
Carr of York, John, 80, 139

Castle Bromwich Hall, 158
Castle Howard, 44, 59-63, 159
Chambers, Sir William, 93
Chatsworth, Derbyshire, 11, 44, 45-52
Chawton House, Hampshire, 27
Chenies, Buckinghamshire, 123
Chicheley, Buckinghamshire, 66
Chicksands Priory, 107, 108, 109
Churchill, Sir Winston, 21, 98-9
City livery companies, treasures of, 104
City of London School, 63
Clandon, Surrey, 101
Clark, Sir Kenneth, 95, 96, 98
Clayton Hall, Lancashire, 157
Clegg, David, 67-70
Clewer Park, Berkshire, 161
Clovelly Court, Devon, 161
Coke family of Holkham, 144
Coleshill, Berkshire, 168
Colindale Hospital, Hendon, 81-2
College of Arms, 103
Colville, Lady Cynthia, 32
Colvin, Howard, 109
Compensation Defence Act (1939),
    14, 174-8
Compton Verney, Warwickshire, 166
Compton Wynyates, Warwickshire, 99
compulsory purchases, 170-1
Convent of the Assumption, 58-9
Cooper, Lady Diana, 22, 27, 119
Cork and Orrery, Earls of, 140
Cornwell Manor, Oxfordshire, 79
Corsham Hall, Wiltshire, 79-80
Country Life articles, 11, 63-4, 65-6
Courtauld Institute Gallery, 87
Coventry, bombing of, 98
Cozens, Air Commodore Henry, 148
Craigmont School, Edinburgh, 42
Crawford, Lord, 102
Crevar, General, 146
Crichel Down, Dorset, 44, 133, 172
Crossrigg Hall, Cumberland, 77-8
Crossman, Richard, 124
Crosswood, near Aberystwyth, 96
Culverthorpe, Lincolnshire, 168

Dalmeny, Scotland, 162
Dalton, Hugh, 125
Dashwood family, 87-9, 149-50
Davenport family, 15
De Havilland, Captain Geoffrey, 150
De Trafford family, 162

Deedes, William, 159
Deene Park, Northamptonshire, 145, 158
Defence Act (1842), 14
Delmer, Sefton, 124
Denham Lodge, Buckinghamshire, 15
Devonshire, Dowager Duchess of, 48-9
Devonshire, Duchess of, 46, 48-9
Devonshire, 10th Duke of, 11, 44-5,
    46, 48-9
Dinton House, 133
Doddington Hall, Cheshire, 166
Domesday Book, 100, 102
Dowding, Lord, 149
Down House, Dorset, 161
Downton Hall, Shropshire, 66-70
Driberg, Tom, 148
Drumlanrig, Scotland, 44, 165
Drysdale, Merida, 101
Duff, Sir Michael, 79
Duke of Wellington's Regiment, 10th
    Battalion, 137-8
Dunorlen Park, Kent, 166
Dutton, Ralph, 43-4, 171-2

East End of London evacuees, 22, 26-7
East Surrey Regiment, 70th Battalion,
    135
Easton, Lincolnshire, 157
Eaton Hall, Cheshire, 150-1
Edmondthorpe, Leicestershire, 162
Edmunds, Charles, 89, 90, 91, 94-5
Egginton Hall, Derbyshire, 157, 164
Eisenhower, General Dwight, 151,
    152
Elgin Regiment of Canada, 147
Elizabeth, Princess (now Queen), 28
Elizabeth, Queen (now Queen
    mother), 28
Elliott, Archibald, 162
Elton Hall, 44, 169
English Heritage, 158
Enigma (German ciphers), 110-11
Enniskillen Cherry Pickers, 136
Evans, Sir David, 101-2

Faringdon House, Berkshire, 145-6
Farnley Hall, Yorkshire, 80
Faulkener, Herbert, 14
Fazackerly, Lancashire, 147
Felix Hall, Essex, 161
Finedon Hall, Northamptonshire, 145
Fitzwilliam family, 136, 137, 138, 139, 142

Foots Cray, Kent, 150
Ford Castle, Northumberland, 73
Foreign Office, 108, 171; Political
    Intelligence Division (CHQ), 2,
    108, 112-27
Fothergill, Brian, 139
Fox, Charles James, 108
Frazer, Mary, 42-3
Free Czech troops, 145, 167
Free French, 145
Froxfield House, 107, 113, 114

Garendon, Leicestershire, 157
George VI, King, 14, 28, 36, 121, 123
Glenfinnan House, 153
Gopsal, Leicestershire, 157
Gordon, Lt-Colonel E.B., 113, 117,
    122, 123
Government Communications HQ,
    Bletchley Park, 14
Greaves, Major, 145
Green Howards, 11th Battalion, 135
Grenadier Guards, 140-2, 165-6; 1st
    Battalion, 140-1
Greystoke Castle, Cumberland, 167
Gunby, Lincolnshire, 13-14

Haddon Hall, Derbyshire, 100-1
Haigh Hall, near Wigan, 102-3
Hake, Sir Henry, 85, 89-93, 94
Hamilton, Lord Claud, 36
Hampton Court Palace, 85, 93, 98
Hanslope House, 107, 108, 109
Harewood, Earl of, 11, 36, 73, 78
Harewood House, 11, 73, 78-9
Harlaxton Manor, Lincolnshire, 148
Harpswell, Lincolnshire, 162
Harris, Sir Arthur 'Bomber', 149
Harrow School, 63, 112
Hartington, Marquess of, 47
Haselbech Hall, 135, 136
Hatfield House, 1, 11, 15, 73-4
Hawkstone Park, Shropshire, 77
Heath House, Staffordshire, 74-5
Heber-Percy, Robert and Jennifer, 146
Hellens, Much Marcle, 158
The Hemplow, Welford, 136
Henley Hall, Shropshire, 86
Herbert family of Pixton Park, 25
Hewlings, Dr Patrick, 137-9
Higgs, William, 123
Highfield House, 136

Hinton Ampner, 43-4, 171-2
Hoare family, 141
Holkham, Norfolk, 144-5
Holland House, London, 159
Hollis, Anne, 60-2
Howard, Sir Algar, 103
Howard, George, 63
Howard, Mariegold Fitzalan, 76
Howard of Glossop, Lord, 73
Hughenden Manor, 149
Hughes family of Kinmel Hall, 81
Hurstmonceaux Castle, Sussex, 171
Hussey, Christopher, 64, 65-6

Ilchester, Lord, 13
Imperial Communications Advisory
    Committee, 12, 112-13
Ingrams, Leonard, 125
intelligence agencies, 107-27
Intelligence Corps depot, 137, 139
Inverailort House, Loch Ailort, 152
Inverary Castle, 153
Isham family, 136
Ismay, Mrs Constance, 135, 136
Italian PoWs, 167

Joicey, Lord, 73

Kay, H.I., 89
Kedleston, 167
Kenwood, Hampstead, 99
Kibblethwaite, A.R., 135
Kinmel Hall, Wales, 81-2
Knole, Kent, 158
Knowsley, 170
Knox, Monsignor Ronald, 58, 59
Korda, Alexander, 21

Lamport Hall, 135-6
Lancing College, 63
Langholm, Scotland, 165
Lawson family, 161
Laydene House, near Petersfield, 150
Lea Castle, Wiltshire, 162
Leeds Castle, Kent, 73
Leeper, Rex, 123
Lees-Milne, James, 79, 80, 86, 88, 100,
    136, 141, 145, 146, 148, 153, 159,
    163-4, 166-9
Leicester, 3rd Earl of, 144
Leicestershire Regiment, 6th
    Battalion, 135

Index

Lennox-Boyd, Alan, 122
Levens Hall, Westmorland, 173
Lichfield, Bishop of, 74
Lichfield, 1st Earl of, 161
Lichfield, Earl and Countess of, 75
Lilleshall, Staffordshire, 27
Lincolnshire, Marquess of, 149
Lingfield Manor, Sussex, 134
Linnean Society, 104
Lisburne, Earl of, 96
Llewylln, Major, 141
London Museum, 99-100
London synagogues, treasures of, 100
Longford Castle, Wiltshire, 133, 162
Longleat, 1, 44, 52-7
Longstowe, 44
Loudon Castle, Ayrshire, 162
Lowther Castle, Westmorland, 133, 157, 169
Lulworth, Dorset, 133
Lyme Park, Cheshire, 28
Lynford Park, Norfolk, 77

MacDonald, Malcolm, 21-2
MacLaren, Neil, 97
Malvern School, 63-6, 112
Manod slate quarry, 99
Mansfield, Earl of, 42
Marlborough House, 29, 37
Marlborough School, 63
Margaret, Princess, 28
Marks Hall, Essex, 159-60
Marlborough, Duke of, 63, 64
Marlborough House, London, 29
Marston House, Somerset, 140, 165
Mary, Queen, 57, 29-37, 120
Medmenham Abbey, 109
Melbury Park, Dorset, 13
Melford Hall, Suffolk, 162
Mells, Somerset, 27, 53, 140; Manor House, 158
Mentmore, Buckinghamshire, 89-95
Menzies, General Sir Stewart ('C'), 109
Mersham le Hatch, Kent, 161
Merton Hall, Norfolk, 2
Methley Hall, Yorkshire, 157
MI5 offices, Blenheim, 112
Miles, Captain Philip, 134
Milnes-Gaskell, Constance, 34
Ministry of Aircraft Production, 98, 99
Ministry of Defence, 108
Ministry of Food, 45

Ministry of Health, 6, 7-8, 13, 22, 80
Ministry of Transport, 6, 8
Minto House, Roxburghshire, 42
Mitford, Nancy, 88, 89, 145
Molyneux, Sir Richard, 36, 37
Money, James, 25-6
Montacute, Somerset, 99
Montague-Stuart-Wortley, Lady Diana, 138
Montgomery, Field Marshal Bernard, 2
Montgomery-Massingberd, Field Marshal, 13
Mount Edgecumbe, Cornwall, 158-9
Muncaster Castle, Cumberland, 99
Munich crisis (September 1938), 6, 7, 29, 86, 89, 97, 100

Naphill, High Wycombe, 149
National Gallery, 89, 95-9, 102
National Library of Wales, 96, 99
National Portrait Gallery, 85, 89-95, 99
National Trust, 14, 87, 99, 100, 141, 148, 149, 167, 168, 170
Natural History Museum, 100
Naworth Castle, 63
Netley Park, Surrey, 168
Newlands railway tunnel, 85
Newsells Park, Hertfordshire, 162
Newton, Lord, 28
Newton Ferrers, Cornwall, 161
Nicolson, Harold, 21
Norfolk, 15th Duke of, 143
Norfolk, 16th Duke of, 140, 143
Normandy landings (1944), 2, 151-2
Normann, E.N. de, 5, 6, 7, 8, 12
North, Doreen (née Douglas), 47-8, 50, 51, 52
North Cray, Kent, 162
North Irish Horse, 136
Northampton, Marquess of, 99
Nuneham Park, near Oxford, 109
Nunney, Somerset, 140

Old Manor House, Hartley Wintney, 147
Old Rectory, Eversholt, 107, 113, 114
Oldbury Hall, Warwickshire, 162
Onslow, Earl of, 101
Oratory School, Reading, 63
Orr, Flying Officer W.R., 149

Paine, James, 80, 166-7

Parham Park, Sussex, 16, 134
Paris House, Woburn, 107, 113, 114
The Park, Wimpole, 79
Patton, General, 142
Pearson, Clive, 134
Pembroke, Earl and Countess of, 142
Pennington-Ramsden family, 99
Penrhos College, 45-52
Penrhyn Castle, 95-9
Peover Hall, Cheshire, 142
Petworth, Sussex, 147
Picton Castle, Wales, 77
Pitchford Hall, Shropshire, 28
Pitreavie Castle, Fife, 152
Pixton Park, Dulverton, Somerset, 25
Plas-y-Bryn, Bontnewydd, 96
Polish soldiers, 145, 167
Pope-Hennessy, James, 30, 34
Port Lympne, Kent, 167
Portal, Sir Charles, 149
Portland, 5th Duke of, 104
Portsmouth Day School for Girls, 43-4
Portsmouth Royal Dockyard, 43, 150, 151
Pratt, Sir Roger, 168
Preston Hall, Kent, 77
Princess Royal, 36, 73, 78
Public Record Office, 100-2

Queen Margaret's School, 59-63

RAF, 147-50, 162, 167-8;
    Bomber Command, 148, 149;
    Fighter Command, 149;
    Photographic Intelligence
    department, 109
Raglan, Lord, 33
Ramridge House, Hampshire, 149
Ramsay, Admiral, 151
Rawlins, Ian, 96, 98, 99
Red House, Bodicote, 14
Red Lynch, Wiltshire, 140
Redgrave, Suffolk, 157
Redhayes, near Exeter, 149
Requisitioned Land War Works Act
    (1945), 170-1
Rhianva, Anglesey, 103
Rigmaden Park, Westmorland, 157, 164
RN schools, 150, 151, 153, 171
Roehampton Convent, London, 173
Rosebery, Lord, 89, 162
Rosneath Castle, 152-3, 170

Rossall School, 63
Rothschild family, 100
Roughwood Park, 14-15
Rouse-Boughton family, 66-7
Royal collections, 93, 98
Royal family, evacuation of the, 28-37
Royal Naval College, Dartmouth, 151
Royal Navy, 150-1, 152-3
Royal Observatory, 171
Royal School, Bath, 52-7
Royal Zoological Society, 103-4
Rufford Abbey, 157, 167
Russell, Conrad, 22-3, 27, 53, 119-22, 140-1
Russell, Gilbert, 140
Russell, Captain the Hon. Leopold, 12, 112-13
Russell, Marjorie, 121
Russell, family vault, Chenies, 123
Rutland, Duke of, 100-1
Rutzen, Sheilda de, 163
Rysbrack, Michael, 35

Sackville-West, Eddie, 87
Salisbury, 4th Marquess of, 11, 15, 73-4
Salisbury Hall, near St Albans, 150
Salvin, Anthony, 77
Samuel, Mrs Osborne, 123
Sandhill Park, Somerset, 77
Sandling Park, Kent, 159
Sandringham, 29, 31
Sassoon, Sir Philip, 167, 171
schools, 12, 22, 41-70; boys' public, 63-6; girls', 11, 44-63, 172; prep, 66-70
Scone Palace, 42, 44
Scott, Adrian Gilbert, 159
Seaton Delaval, Northumberland, 135
Sheffield, 50-1
Shepton Mallet gaol, 102
Shillinglee Park, Sussex, 162
Shobrooke, Devon, 161
Shrewsbury, Earls of, 167
Shrewsbury School, 63
Shugborough, Staffordshire, 161
Sir John Soane's Museum, 102-3
Sitwell, Osbert, 30, 35-7
Sizergh Castle, 173
Slebach, Wales, 163-4
Slindon, Sussex, 163
Smedmore, Dorset, 133

Snell, Dr W.E. and Mrs, 80-2
Somerleyton, Suffolk, 79
South Saskatchewan Regiment, 147
Southern Command HQ, Wilton, 2, 133, 142
Southwick Park/House, 2, 151-2, 171
Speaker's House portraits, 93
Special Intelligence Service, 109-11
Stansted Park, Sussex, 146-7
Stapleford Park, Leicestershire, 77
Stockeld Park, Yorkshire, 80
Stockwood Park, Bedfordshire, 80
Stoke Ferry Hall, Norfolk, 159
Stourhead, 133, 140, 141
Stowe School, 64
Stuart, 'Athenian', 161
Stuart, Sir Campbell, 113, 114, 117, 122, 123
Sudbourne, Suffolk, 157
Sudely Castle, Gloucestershire, 99
Sunderlandwick Hall, Yorkshire, 162
Sunninghill Park, Berkshire, 142
Supreme Allied Command, HQ, Southwick Park, 2, 151-2
Swainston, Isle of Wight, 158

Tate Gallery, 99
Tattershall Castle, Lincolnshire, 100
Thompson, Francis, 49
Thornbury Castle, 103
Torbock family, 77-8
Trent Park, Hertfordshire, 171
Trinity House, 104
Tullichewan Castle, 153
Tyneham, Dorset, 133

Ultra (code-breaker), 110-11
USAAF, 147, 149

Van der Elst, Mrs, 148
Van Dyck, Sir Anthony, 95, 96, 98
Vansittart, Lord, 125
Vaynol, North Wales, 79
Verney, Sir Harry, 103
Victoria & Albert Museum, 99
The Vyne, Hampshire, 66

WAAFs, 143
Waddesden Manor, 41
Wakehurst Place, Surrey, 146
Wallace Collection, 87-8
Walrond family, 79

War Damage Commission, 159, 170
War Graves Commission cemetery, Hatfield Park, 74
War Office, 6, 8, 13, 108, 133-4
Warcop Hall, 133
Warnford Park, Hampshire, 157
Warren House, Hertfordshire, 80
Watlington Hall, Norfolk, 162
Waugh, Evelyn, vii-viii, 23-5, 86-7, 132, 160-1, 174
Webb, John, 166
Websters of Kendal, 164
Welbeck Abbey, 104
Wells, H.G., 21
Wentworth Woodhouse, 136-40, 142
West Park, Hampshire, 162
West Wycombe Park, 87-9, 149-50, 166
Westminster, Dukes of, 151
Westminster School, 63
Westwood Bath Stone Quarries, 94, 99
Weymouth Lady, 27
Wickham, Major, 32
Wilkins, William, 162
Williams, Valentine, 125
Williams-Ellis, Clough, 131
Wilton House, 2, 133, 142
Wimborne, Lord, 135
Windsor Castle, 28-9
Winstanley Hall, Lancashire, 169-70
Witt, Sir Robert, collection of, 87
Woburn Abbey, 1, 2, 15-16, 17-18, 103-4, 107, 108, 112-27, 137, 164, 170
Woodcote, near Henley, 63
Woodfold Park, Lancashire, 157
Woodhall Park, Hertfordshire, 66
Woolton, Lord, 34
Wooton, Surrey, 161
Worcestershire Regiment, 135-6; 11th Battalion, 135
WRNS, 125, 150, 153
WVS, 26
Wyatt, Samuel, 166
Wyatt, Thomas Henry, 135
Wycombe Abbey, 149
Wyndham, Maggie, 33

York, Duke and Duchess of, 142
York Military Hospital, 73, 76-7